Old New York in Picture Postcards

1900–1945

Jack H. Smith

Lanham ◆ New York ◆ Oxford

VESTAL PRESS, Inc.

Published in the United States of America
by Vestal Press, Inc.
4720 Boston Way
Lanham, Maryland 20706

Copyright © by Vestal Press, Inc.

Library of Congress Cataloging-in-Publication Data

Smith, Jack H.
    Old New York in picture postcards, 1900–1945 / Jack H. Smith.
        p.   cm.
    Includes bibliographical references and index.
    ISBN 1-879511-43-6 (pbk. : alk. paper)
    1. New York (N.Y.)—History—1898–1951 Pictorial works. 2. New York (N.Y.)—
Social life and customs—20th century Pictorial works. 3. Architecture—New York (State)—New York—
History—20th century Pictorial works. 4. Postcards—New York (State)—New York. I. Title.
F128.5.S65 1999
974.7′104—dc21   99-21467
                                                                                                              CIP

♾ ™The paper used in this publication meets the minimum requirements of
American National Standard for Information Sciences—Permanence of
Paper for Printed Library Materials, ANSI/NISO Z39.48—1992.
Manufactured in the United States of America.

Contents

Introduction

Of all the world's great cities—in both ancient times and our own modern era—New York is clearly and easily the most ethnically diverse. Which means, as well, that it is the most culturally diverse of all communities. Which, in turn, makes it the most interesting of towns.

Within the boundaries of its five boroughs (Manhattan, Brooklyn, Queens, Staten Island, and the Bronx) dozens of languages and dialects may be heard, the voices often belonging to people who live in regional enclaves of like-minded and like-sounding individuals. Manhattan's Little Italy and Chinatown are two of the more well-known, but there are several other such minicommunities.

Among the things this diversity has created is an atmosphere of tolerance and acceptance of the best that each citizen within each group can contribute to the city. Also created, because of this acceptance, is a delightful variety in everything from art to architecture, cuisine to entertainment. In such an environment one should not be surprised to encounter an exciting array of sights and sounds not to be found in quite the same way, or to quite the same degree, anywhere else.

Need examples? What other city has witnessed two world's fairs in twenty-five years (1939 and 1964)? Where else could that archetype of entertainment venue, Coney Island, have been constructed? What other city could have designed that model of urban leisure and recreation, Central Park? Where else would Wall Street, the financial center of the universe, be more appropriately located? In what other city could "Broadway," that theatrical mecca, be placed? Where else but in New York would one look for the world's busiest harbors, the world's greatest subway transportation system, the tallest buildings, finest restaurants, best museums, most prestigious stores?

And where else but in Gotham would one expect to find the headquarters for the fashion industry, the telecommunications industry, the printing industry, and the advertising industry?

If America is an experiment in democracy, New York must be the most visible example of the fruits that democracy can produce. Which doesn't quite forgive the occasional rudeness one encounters from some New Yorkers—though it certainly goes some distance toward explaining the genesis of that smugness. Humility might, after all, be somewhat unnatural in that milieu. Which also explains why most of New York's millions wouldn't live anywhere else.

Who can blame them?

Like every other city on earth, New York has a history that includes successes and failures, excellence and excess. It is a story of the great and the infamous, of political integrity and political corruption, of architectural splendor and poor urban development.

In truth, all of this and more (the tale is an intriguing one) could have been expected from a city that has often underestimated its own growth potential—or, in some cases, underestimated the intelligence and the ingenuity of its citizenry. The cast of characters who made the city what it is may be seen in two lights: Rogue's Gallery and Hall of Fame. Diamond Jim, "Boss" Tweed, Stanford White, Fiorello La Guardia. And more: Astors, Vanderbilts, Rockefellers, Roosevelts.

Again, the key to understanding New York City is to recognize its diversity—diversity with an ethnic flavor, diversity with a social component, diversity in architecture, in neighborhoods, in cuisine, in entertainment venues. In anything and everything. And yet there is unity. A lot of it. Everyone goes to Macy's, to Central Park, to Rockefeller Center. Everyone complains about the cab service, about the garbage strikes, about slow-moving tourists. All New Yorkers refuse to be impressed by most things in the city, and by absolutely nothing outside of it.

They may not know their history as well as they should, but they do know it is impressive. They also know that it has been oft told, the characters oft described. So why another history, even if it is a delightfully illustrated one? Answer: With such a topic, such a city, the story is worth retelling, the characters worth another description, another look-see.

Then another.

WHY POSTCARDS?

For more than 125 years, picture postcards have served as cameras, visual recording devices, permitting us glimpses of the natural world and its multiple inhabitants. They have freeze-framed, as well, everything that is man-made, bringing it into focus for our perusal.

When postcards first came into use (during the 1860s, as government postals), their immediate popularity and ready acceptance assured their longevity as rapid communication tools. Their continued use was indeed guaranteed given one crucial reality: Postcards were time savers. No longer compelled to purchase both envelopes and writing paper, correspondents now needed only to scribble a few lines on these pieces of rectangular paperboard, and their task of communicating with friends and relatives was complete, leaving time for more pleasurable pursuits.

Even writing the phrase "Wish You Were Here" was often unnecessary, as many picture postcards had that message already planted on the card's front. And what amount of prose could seriously hope to compete with the card's two- and three-dimensional images, frequently splashed with vividly delicious colors?

In fact, the cards themselves became immensely popular as collectibles. For a brief period (ca. 1895–1915) picture postcards were reputed to be the world's most ardently collected item. The fad extended to staid old Queen Victoria, who maintained an album, a reflection of a taste that had so totally captivated her subjects. The popularity itself was grist for the producers' mill as they added more and more views to their offerings.

Moreover, during the past two decades, picture postcards have become godsends to those wishing to reconstruct the past. As chroniclers of the bygone, they are nonpareil. Whether the object of investigation is politics, war, location views, or 101 other things, postcards are firsthand, first-rate history. Displaying everything from art and architecture to styles of dress and natural phenomena, millions of individual postcards are available to Show It Like It Was.

And when that examination involves a city like New York, the views one will encounter are nothing short of fascinating. They are also seemingly endless: street scenics of the Long Ago showing attire, means of transportation, retail establishments, all forever gone; an uncrowded Central Park, leisurely enjoyed; once-familiar landmarks existing now only in memory—and on picture postcards; bridges, hotels, restaurants, captured in a moment, framed for all time; Coney Island in its heyday; world's fairs revisited.

As the viewers of this book inspect these cards, they will have ample visible evidence of where our ancestors have been. More important, they will see how the city of New York traveled the distance in time from where it was to where it is. They will also develop an appreciation for the postcard and come to realize why this particular journey—and many others—is best taken aboard the postcard as the means of conveyance—because the card has already made the trip.

Why the postcard?

Why indeed.

CHAPTER 1

Purchasing Manhattan

When Dutch trader, leader, and entrepreneur Peter Minuit obtained Manhattan Island from the Algonquin Indians for the princely sum of sixty guilders' (the equivalent of twenty-four dollars') worth of trinkets, he could not have known that the world's most fascinating metropolis would later rise from the soil of that location.

In many ways the most exciting city on earth, New York is easily the one with the most human variety as well. Almost 8 million people, speaking dozens of languages and inhabiting ethnic communities scattered randomly across the city's landscape, dwell within the boundaries of its five boroughs.

In those early seventeenth-century days New Amsterdam, as it was called by its Dutch occupants, comprised only the lower end of the island of Man-a-hat-ta (land of hills); Brooklyn, Queens, the Bronx, and Staten Island did not unite with Manhattan until 1898 to form the New York City we know today.

The founder's wall designed to prevent successful attacks on the city was later to become the beginning of a road, one that retained, in name at least, its historical significance. It became Wall Street, the financial center of human economic activity.

Peter Minuit would be more than surprised.

Emigrant Landing

2013—
Emigrant
Landing,
New York.

Souvenir Post Card Co. New York and Berlin

Though America's eastern and western shores are unlike in many ways, they do share one important element in common: Both were points of arrival for millions of immigrants. Los Angeles, San Francisco, and Seattle witnessed an influx of Asians and citizens of the Pacific Rim Basin. For New York the reality was somewhat different.

Eastern Europeans, Western Europeans, Asians, Australians, Latin Americans, and more: They came—and still come—from every corner of the globe, disembarking at New York's harbors and airports. For them New York represents the American Dream and did so long before the Statue of Liberty "lifted her lamp beside the golden door."

Ellis Island and Emigrant Landing were the first steps to a new life in a new world. And though the waiting line was sure to be long and the buildings cramped for space, the promise of a new start infused the sometimes haggard and dirty faces with hope.

Often their first neighborhood surroundings in America were foul smelling, dimly lit, and squalorly inhospitable. No matter—New York offered opportunity, which is what they came for. Most of these new arrivals accepted another fact: Where they wound up, and what they eventually became, depended in large measure, if not solely, upon themselves.

The West Street and North River Piers

The West Street and North River Piers, New York City.

©American Studio, N. Y.

The later view of West Street and the North (Hudson) River piers shows the physical proximity of the street, the railroad, and the river. The sight of the trains and the ships, along with the motor traffic passing down the street itself, gives some indication of the level of activity in the area even more than sixty years ago.

Like much of the rest of New York City, West Street has a fascinating history. Its creation was made possible in the second decade of the nineteenth century when the riverbank was extended and raised so that docks might be built. By 1890 it had displaced South Street in the Lower East Side (running parallel to the East River) as the main gateway for waterborne traffic. Located along its thoroughfare was the twenty-three-story West Street Building, with its decorative chimneys and gables; the watch museum of Fred W. Jensen and Son; the New York Telephone Company Building; and the Phoenix Foundry, where, in the 1830s, Captain John Ericsson designed and constructed with the use of screw propellers America's first iron sailing boats and steamships.

The lower end of West Street today fronts New York's tallest, if not most impressive, building—the twin-towered World Trade Center.

West Street Looking North

Copyright 1905 by the Rotograph Co.
A 183. West St. looking North, N. Y. City.

This early scenic of West Street in lower Manhattan belies the road's importance. The commercial significance of West Street, which runs parallel to the Hudson River on the Lower East Side, is hard to overstate. By 1940 its function as a main gateway for waterborne traffic rendered its value in the half-million-dollar-an-acre range, with a pier value of fifteen hundred dollars per linear foot. Given the relative worth of a dollar in the years prior to World War II, it is easy to ascertain the value of this prime piece of real estate.

As reflected on this card, pre-1910 American cities had broad, unpaved streets with little motor-vehicular traffic. West Street, even by this standard, was wider than most avenues, and for good reason. Freight being loaded onto, and off of, ships, trains, and wagons was an ongoing transaction that increased in activity and tonnage with the passage of years. That level of activity demanded a wide thoroughfare.

Indeed, by the time asphalt and cement replaced packed earth and wooden planks, the flow of commerce along West Street was so great that it rivaled Times Square in bustle and bluster, profanity and awe.

Broadway North from Ann Street

E-1224. Broadway North from Ann Street, New York, N. Y.

Even before the Bank of New York opened its doors in 1784, the city had been a center of considerable commercial activity. Since the mid 1800s its economic growth has at times been geometric rather than arithmetic.

Almost every category of economic activity imaginable exists within New York environs. The fashion/garment business ranks at the top, but publishing, advertising, printing, public relations, food products, banking, brokerage and commodity houses, electrical equipment, the entertainment business, and other enterprises all conduct brisk business in or from their New York locations.

Manhattan is the center for more than half the city's manufacturing—not a surprising fact, given its central shipping site and its proximity to Wall Street.

This pre-1920 vignette of Broadway, replete with pedestrian traffic, picturesque streetcars, and other types of transport, shows a city very much "on the move," an accurate description of Manhattan if ever one existed.

Seventh Avenue, North of 125th Street

Seventh Avenue, North of One Hundred and Twenty-fifth Street, New York.

Originally established in 1658 by Peter Stuyvesant, Nieuw Haarlem (New Harlem) was a peaceful Hollander village with farms named Quiet Vale and Happy Valley. Located on the west side of the Harlem River and north of Central Park, Harlem has developed three distinct enclaves today: Spanish Harlem, Italian Harlem, and Black Harlem. The first and last mentioned have become known even to those who have never been to New York.

Before 1900 the Germans, Irish, Jews, and Italians were Harlem's dominant ethnic groups, and the neighborhood was a fashionable one, as befits an area adjoining New York's famous Polo Grounds.

Seventh Avenue is Harlem's widest street and is lined with various service types of business, from beauty parlors to restaurants. One Hundred Twenty-fifth Street is also a busy commercial street, witnessing teeming throngs of pedestrian traffic.

Steel Girder for New Municipal Building

Among the items that future historians will record about the twentieth century is its propensity for erecting massive buildings often boastfully—and erroneously—referred to as "skyscrapers." This "bigger is more impressive if not better" concept was every bit as prevalent at the beginning of this century as it is while we await its closing.

New York's forty-story municipal building, erected in 1914 by the ubiquitous firm of McKim, Mead, and White, towers over nearby city hall. The top roof section, ten stories in height, is an invigorating sight, with its towers and peaks and the equally impressive Civic Fame statue residing aloft. Adolph Alexander Weinman, known to legions of numismatists as the designer of the "Mercury" dime, was also the creator of this gilt,

heroic figure, as well as of the relief work on the lower part of the building.

The intermediate stories have been described as dignified, but it has also been suggested in various quarters that the Corinthian colonnade at the building's base would have been more ideally suited for a smaller structure.

Looking at the completed building, one finds it difficult to conceptualize the dimensions of some of the materials and individual units of which it is made. The steel girder shown here weighed 120,000 pounds, necessitating its being placed on a hundred-ton truck, which was in turn pulled by a team of twenty horses. Make that twenty tired horses.

125th Street Looking East
from Park Avenue

2082—125th Street, looking East from Park Avenue, NEW YORK.

Looking east from Park Avenue on 125th Street is gazing in the direction of Harlem. In fact, 125th Street was—and still is—one of the most commercially active thoroughfares running through Harlem. The artery feeds into the Triborough Bridge, a Y-shaped affair connecting Manhattan with Queens and the Bronx at the time of its opening in 1936. The bridge's overall length of 17,710 feet was exceeded only by the San Francisco–Oakland Bridge. However, the Triborough was not one continuous span, as it actually comprised four bridges over the water and twelve bridges over land.

(Both the Triborough and the San Francisco bridges have been dwarfed by four concrete trestles, all located in Louisiana.)

Hyde Statue, Equitable Life Building

Alex Marburger, 17 Ann Street, New York.

No 3. Hyde Statue. Equitable Life Building. New York. Destroyed by Fire. January 9th. 1912.

No city in America has managed to escape the ravages of fire. New York is, unhappily, not an exception to this rule. Nor have all of New York's fires been of the home-owner or slum-infested-area variety, as this postcard attests.

As is also painfully clear from this picture, the business of building skyscrapers was not followed by sufficient improvements in municipal fire-fighting departments to meet the need should such a structure ignite.

The Equitable Life Building fire of January 9, 1912, took place on a Tuesday morning in the heart of the Wall Street district. The securities of several hundred people, valued later at between 500 million and 1 billion 1912 dollars, lay buried under its ruins. Fortunately, those securities were locked inside fireproof vaults the equal of those used in San Francisco at the time of the great earthquake in that city in 1906.

In both cases the securities and other important papers were intact.

The Big Equitable Fire

WATER TOWER IN ACTION   NEW YORK.

THE
Big Equitable Fire.

One interesting phenomenon relating to the Equitable fire is the alarm that it *did not* occasion in New York's financial community. The market reasoned that securities in a fireproof vault would be, as they ought to be, secure.

Not only the San Francisco earthquake but other earlier conflagrations had proved the safety of such vaults.

Furthermore, even if something did go awry, both the stock exchange through closure and the federal courts through temporary nonenforcement of contracts and deliveries would protect the aforementioned securities. With such measures are the wealthy shielded from loss by natural disaster. For the rich it is a matter of rebuilding—for the poor, of starting over with only what they can carry away.

Proof of this was shortly forthcoming. In 1914 the New Equitable Building, designed by E. R. Graham, was constructed to a height of forty-one stories and contained 1.2 million square feet of rentable floor space. For more than twenty-five years it was the second-largest building in floor space in the city.

Elevated Railroad on the Bowery

9312 — Elevated Railroad on Bowery, New York

If any part of Manhattan may be said to be truly immune to change, that area would have to be a slice of Manhattan's Lower East Side, the Bowery district. The Bowery's seedy reputation has been enhanced by movies, books, and popular imagination.

Make no mistake: Much of that reputation is well deserved. Derelicts, drug addicts (and pushers), street peddlers, and unsavory characters of all types inhabit the street itself—as do discount stores and flea markets.

But there is also the Silver Palace restaurant, with its blinking-eyed dragons and Chinese decor, and the Bowery Savings Bank, its massive classical columns and sculpture-filled pediment making it one of the most elegant bank buildings in America.

Bowery and Doubledeck Elevated RR

Bowery and Doubledeck Elevated R. R.,
New York City.

More than thirty years before New York began construction on its enviable subway system, the elevated railway was devised to alleviate the traffic flow on New York's increasingly crowded streets.

Charles T. Harvey's genius was responsible for the planning. It called for the trains to be raised to at least thirty feet above street level, running on steel-braced tracks. The first was tested on Greenwich Street in 1867.

These Els were drawn by steam engines instead of cable; eventually they extended to the Lower East Side, then crossed the East River into Brooklyn. They were doomed, however, by the noise and pollution they generated—that, and the onslaught of New York's subway system, which beginning in 1904 extended, in time, to every section of Manhattan and beyond.

Hotel Taft

It is sometimes difficult for small-town America to come to grips with the occasional large scale on which New York City exists. Times Square's Hotel Taft provides a good illustration of this point. Within its four multistoried buildings were two thousand rooms, each featuring a radio, many with that newfangled gadget, the TV.

Its interior a combination of futurism and art deco, the Taft contained a coffee shop, tap room, grill, and decorous lobby, each done but scant justice on this postcard.

At the point in time when the Square itself was beginning to deteriorate, perhaps ever so slightly into the garish and the obscene, the Taft could be seen shining brightly with distinction.

Hotel Wentworth

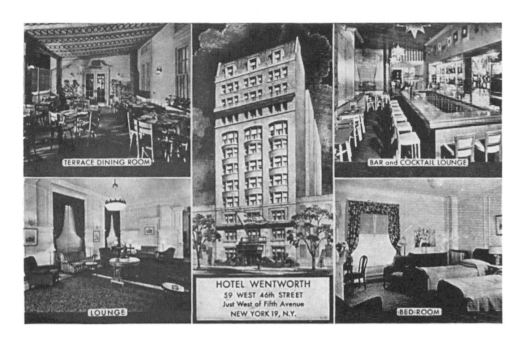

TERRACE DINING ROOM

BAR and COCKTAIL LOUNGE

LOUNGE

HOTEL WENTWORTH
59 WEST 46th STREET
Just West of Fifth Avenue
NEW YORK 19, N.Y.

BED ROOM

Though the Hotel Wentworth is not what it was (few things are), and though the building itself is far from being a dominating presence, New Yorkers may yet be modestly proud that the hotel is still standing.

Built during the art-deco thirties, the Wentworth reflected that style's decor, plainly visible in these vignettes. The period was undeniably an exuberant one, but even on a lesser scale, such as is demonstrated here, an aura of excitement and inventiveness is clearly evident.

In a few years the 1939 New York World's Fair would dominate the scene; then World War II would rear its unsightly head. But before that—and during, and after—hotels like the Wentworth spoke of a time when "tomorrow" did not seem to be a dirty word, but rather a term filled with hope and pleasant surprises.

New Brighton Theatre

New Brighton Theatre, Brighton Beach, N. Y.

This card is testament to a time when Coney Island, Manhattan Beach, and Brighton Beach ruled southern Brooklyn, digging their tentacles of fantasy and delight into the rest of New York—and into America, for that matter.

For all the hucksterism implied here, there was also an appeal to opulence. In addition to entertainment of perhaps sometimes questionable quality and character, there existed on Brighton a resort atmosphere where the wealthy and the privileged enjoyed plush surroundings on their island enclave. This was the presumed distinction between Coney and Brighton: The former was a diversionary neighbor to the latter, its raucous behavior and commoner trappings easily avoided by retreat to more exclusive surroundings.

Even Europe's Marienbad, that spa with amenities for the privileged few, could not outglitter Brooklyn's Manhattan and Brighton beaches.

Sheepshead Bay

17. SHEEPSHEAD BAY. BROOKLYN, N. Y.

Named for the fish that once inhabited its waters in vast numbers, Brooklyn's Sheepshead Bay was, and is, well-known both for its excellent deep-sea fishing and for the equally excellent seafood restaurants that line its shore. There were also entertainment and sporting venues, such as the racetrack featured on this postcard, a concession to the proximity of Sheepshead Bay to Coney Island.

Sheepshead today is a mixture of the old and the new, with the new, unfortunately, dominating. There are a few remaining nice touches, however. The Wycoff-Bennet residence, with its picket fence and six-columned porch, is arguably the most aesthetically appealing of Brooklyn's Dutch-style homes. Also of merit is the Elias Ryder home on 28th Street, a Dutch colonial rose in Brooklyn's garden of hybrids.

New York, Morningside Park

New York. Morning Side Park.

Bros.

This early-twentieth-century view of Morningside Park reveals a pastoral setting in what one would have imagined was a safe, secure environment. That may have been true then; it is less so now.

This is an especial shame given the overall grandeur of the area, which includes Morningside Heights and Riverside Drive. History abounds in this locale, which was, among other things, the site of a Revolutionary War skirmish.

Designed by Central Park's Olmsted and Vaux, Morningside Park was opened in 1887 (three years before Riverside Drive) and was well utilized for decades af-ter that time. Today it is Morningside Heights rather than Morningside Park, which lends itself to pedestrian traffic that is oft trod upon. It's easy to see why. Cultural and historical institutions are scattered about the area, which also boasts splendid, sometimes intriguing, residential architecture: Columbia University, St. Paul's Chapel, Buell Hall (last remnant of the Bloomingdale Insane Asylum), the Roman Catholic Eglise de Notre Dame, St. Luke's Hospital, Amsterdam House, and St. John the Divine Church.

And much more. It's a pleasing view of Manhattan in decked-out fashion. And, if one's legs are solid, it's an inexpensive tour in the bargain.

Fire Boat, New York

FIRE BOAT "NEW YORKER"
AT THE BATTERY, NEW YORK

Before the construction of Central Park made that location New York's area of recreational egalitarianism, lower Manhattan's Battery Park performed this function in somewhat less pretentious fashion. Gentry and laborer, male and female, dark or light, parasol or without: All could be seen along the waterfront.

Named for the row of British guns stored here during the 1680s, Battery Park has always been a popular site.

Now referred to as Battery Park City, it has become playground, debarkation point, residential area, shopping locale, and, with the many plaques and monuments, a tourist attraction as well. From here one may ferry to the Statue of Liberty or to New Jersey, or walk along wooden piers, enjoying both the waterfront breezes and the magnificent views.

Though the Battery is often crowded, its appeal is felt by natives and visitors alike—just as it was when this fire boat docked here all those decades ago.

Barnard College

Barnard College, N. Y. City

No. 58. National Art Views Co. N. Y. City.

All-female Barnard College, established in 1889, is affiliated with Columbia University both in terms of physical proximity and by cross registration between the two schools. Only females, however, are permitted to be part of Barnard's permanent student body. The institution still cherishes and maintains this aspect of its identity.

Barnard's manicured landscape is a refreshingly welcome sight for those accustomed to inner-city universities that are more in keeping with urban sprawl, with asphalt and concrete abounding. The appearance of its mascot, the bear, on the shield above the 117th Street entrance, is also a nice touch.

More significant is the fact that Barnard's graduates have excelled in almost every form of human endeavor imaginable. This is some distance removed from the time in the 1860s, when Bellevue was willing to accept a few female medical students with the hope that they might be able to master the curriculum.

Barnard College

Another early view of Barnard College. From this angle, taken at a lower level looking up, the build- ing appears taller and more imposing, its brick and limestone seeming to cover a greater area.

Lower Broadway and Staten Island Ferry

Lower Broadway and Staten Island Ferry, New York.

Although the Staten Island Ferry ride is no longer five cents, as it was when this picture was taken, the trip is well worth the increased fare. The view of Ellis Island, as well as those of the Statue of Liberty and lower Manhattan's skyscrapers from the Ferry, are nonpareil.

Once the Island itself is reached, the visitor is presented with another series of views, ones that seem almost pastoral when compared with Manhattan's asphalt. That's because Staten Island is more residential than commercial, more people and culture oriented than business concentrated.

One may take the forty-minute train ride or use one of the borough's buses to drink up some of the Island culture. Sights include the Snug Harbor Cultural Center—an eighty-acre gem that features columned Greek Revival temples—the Newhouse Center for Con-

temporary Art, the Staten Island Botanical Gardens, and a Children's Museum.

Photographer Alice Austen's residence is another visual treat, both for the Dutch-style architecture and for the photographic exhibits within the home.

Even more intriguing is a walk through the ninety-six-acre, twenty-six-building museum village called Richmondtown. It's a history lesson like no other. Richmondtown is also the site of Staten Island's first permanent settlement, and the borough has spared no expense in recreating the appropriate seventeenth-century (1685) atmosphere.

Still scattered among the residential sections of Staten Island are wooded and wetland areas, which are a refreshment all their own.

West Washington Market

West Washington Market. New York.

Although it is obvious that New York is set apart from the rest of America by its giantism, unique history, and architectural splendor, it yet shares much with other towns and cities all across the United States.

One of those similarities can be found on this view card. From Bangor to Portland, farmers, ranchers, craftsmen, fishermen, and other types of entrepreneurs peddled their wares in both open-air arenas and specially con-structed buildings. Anyone who has been to a farmer's market, a flea market, or an auction knows the sense of anticipation experienced by buyer and seller both. Each anticipates the sale, one contemplating profits, the other sharpening negotiating skills in order to obtain a bargain. That atmosphere, the one created by this view, is a universally recognized phenomenon.

Think of being ten years old once more, on your way to the circus or the fair. Now look at this picture again.

Nassau Street North from Liberty Street

Nassau Street North from Liberty Street,
New York City.

Nassau and Liberty are two well-known streets in lower Manhattan. They intersect within a few feet of the New York Federal Reserve Bank, one of the many financial institutions in proximity to Wall and Broad streets (Nassau becomes Broad running north).

Notable area architecture includes the John Street United Methodist Church, the cast-iron Nassau Street (lofts), the splendid beaux-arts former New York State Chamber of Commerce building, and the terra-cotta Liberty Tower.

Nassau has also become a much-foot-traveled Pedestrian Mall featuring specialized stores as well as the unpleasantly ubiquitous chain outlets and discount houses.

Note the headgear worn by all on this postcard, a concession to popular taste in pre-1920 America. Even with the uniformity this practice suggests, one is inclined to see this style as, well, stylish.

Cheerio.

Post Office, New York City

Post Office, New York City.

All too often it is the case that "progress" is defined in terms of demolishing and replacing rather than improving on what has existed previously. It may be argued that the late nineteenth and early twentieth century New York post office seen here suffered just such a fate: It was replaced by a "more appropriate physical plant." Architect William Kendall (who had joined the firm of McKim, Mead, and White in 1906) designed the new building, which had a most mundane name given it in 1918: the U.S. General Post Office.

In 1982 this replacement became known as the James A. Farley Building, Farley having been the fifty-third postmaster general of the United States.

As for the memory of the building shown here? Thank God for postcards.

CHAPTER 2

Statue of Liberty

1 — STATUE OF LIBERTY, NEW YORK CITY

No statue on earth is more easily and readily recognized than the Lady with the Lamp. She does not guard our shores, nor does she bid welcome to all who would make America their home. Those numbers are too great, even for our broad shoulders.

But she does represent all that America represents: waving fields of grain, purple-mountained majesty, streets lined with golden opportunities for the hard worker and the person with vision. All of that, and something else, too: freedom. Freedom to join or not to join, to agree or to disagree, to applaud or to complain. Freedom to grow full measure. Mainly, one supposes, freedom of thought, especially that sort of thought which dares to believe that tomorrow just might be better than today.

Eliciting sentiments like those, why shouldn't she stand proudly against the skyline?

Statue of Liberty at Sunrise

THE STATUE OF LIBERTY AT SUNRISE, NEW YORK CITY

Frederic Auguste Bartholdi designed works other than the Statue of Liberty. But it was she who granted immortality to the Frenchman. Her own recent facelift having been completed in 1986 (one hundred years after her original unveiling), the Lady is now ready for at least another hundred years of national identity.

A few facts about her are in order.

She was a gift of the French people, though it took our own populace a full nine years to raise the necessary capital for building the base. The statue was begun in 1875 and completed in 1886, but not before clay models and plaster-cast fragment enlargements had been rendered. Finally, the projected height of 151 feet was reached. The real statue required wooden molds from full-scale plaster fragments. Onto them were riveted three-hundred sheets of cooper, which were then hammered into conforming shape.

The internal wrought-iron bracing was designed by Gustave Eiffel, who had already procured his reputation a decade earlier with his own monumental tower.

The granite pedestal (ninety-eight feet) and the joining concrete base (sixty-five feet) were designed by American architect Richard Morris Hunt.

The years had mounted from conception to finished product. The Statute of Liberty's unveiling by President Grover Cleveland on Bedloe Island (renamed Liberty Island in 1956) capped off many years of effort.

And of passion.

Clinton Avenue, Brooklyn

Clinton Avenue, Brooklyn, N. Y.

Tree-lined drives, whether in Brooklyn, or Bakersfield, were the order of the day for an America in that time of the Long Ago: a time when automobiles did not spew their poisons, residential architecture was generally pleasing to the eye, and a neighborhood stroll did not include apprehensions about personal safety.

More than just being examined, this view should be cherished, its finer features returned to, the visions it suggests and creates emulated on a grand scale.

New York may have been a "little apple" in those days, but it was surely a cleaner, safer, "peachier" place as well.

Hotel St. George

HOTEL ST. GEORGE,
Brooklyn Heights, N. Y.

Another structure to which Brooklyn's citizens looked with pride was the Hotel St. George. Erected in 1885 (architect: Augustus Hatfield) with later additions (1890–1923, architect: Montrose Morris and others), the St. George covered an entire city block and boasted over twenty-six hundred rooms, making it Brooklyn's largest hotel for a time.

It served as residence both to the borough's natives and visitors, as well as to folk from lower Manhattan. A first-class building outside and in (boasting all the modern amenities as they became available), the St. George's reputation was undiluted to midtwentieth century.

The buildings shown here are now separate entities, each being developed along different lines. Presumably progress on the move.

St. Denis Hotel

VALENTINE-SOUVENIR CO.N.Y

LADIES' AND GENTLEMEN'S GRILL
ST. DENIS HOTEL
BROADWAY AT ELEVENTH STREET, NEW YORK CITY

R. L. CARROLL, PROP.

This 1930s vignette of the Ladies' and Gentlemen's Grill at the St. Denis Hotel could easily move the term "grill" to a more elevated position than it now occupies. White tablecloths; a table setting that included crystal goblets, cloth napkins, and delicately decorated plates; pictures on ornamented walls; wide spacing between tables; even an elegant staircase: This was a clear-cut example of finer dining when that activity was more formal, less hurried, and more gracefully polite.

One wonders if the hotel was dressed so resplendently in 1877 when Alexander Graham Bell came to town and demonstrated his new gadget, the telephone, on the premises of the St. Denis.

Hotel Margaret

For native Brooklynites this postcard view of the Hotel Margaret, its opulence "Overlooking Manhattan and New York Harbor," is a sad reminder of yet another landmark forever gone.

Frank Freeman's creation was destroyed by fire in 1980. The apartment house that replaced it is called, inappropriately, The Margaret. Its psychedelic coloring (green and orange) and post–World War II structuring do not a pleasing effect make. Nor does it reflect the one-time dominance enjoyed by its predecessor.

Cooper Square

611   COOPFR SQUARE, NEW YORK.

This early view of Cooper Square illustrates not only the accelerated pace of living that was well under way in America's larger cities by the turn of the century, but also the sometimes unsightly scenery that accompanied that desire to expand and dominate the landscape.

Peter Cooper, after whom the area was named, was a tough-minded industrialist—a partner of Samuel F. B. Morse in laying the first Atlantic cable—who yet cared enough about the city in which he lived to found in 1859 a college (Cooper Union) devoted to free technical education for the common folk, and also used as a forum for public discourse. A statue of Cooper, sculpted by the eminent Augustus Saint-Gaudens, graces the square to this day.

Cooper Square is vastly improved aesthetically from what is shown here. The Cooper Union Foundation Building, a marvelous Italianate brownstone—which is the oldest building in America framed with steel railroad rails used as beams—is one of many notable structures. One of its fascinations are the interesting exhibits within its three galleries. Also of merit is the Cooper Square Assembly of God (previously the Metropolitan Savings Bank), with its architectural distinctiveness, and the residential apartments in the area, which indicate a neighborhood given to preservation and innovation both.

33

U.S. Sub Treasury

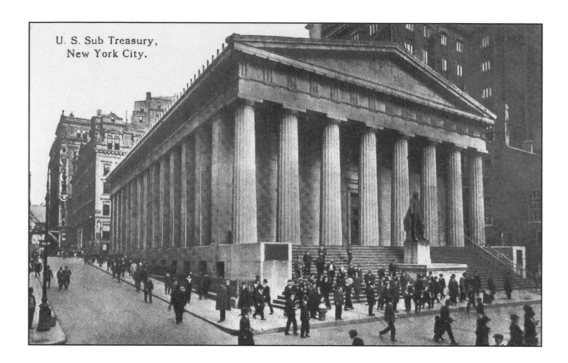

U. S. Sub Treasury,
New York City.

Simple and unadorned, this Doric-columned temple represents the Greek Revival style with small-scale, unpretentious grandeur. Its original use was as the U.S. Custom House (1842–62); later it became the U.S. Sub Treasury (1862–1925) before assuming duty as the Federal Hall National Memorial.

Constructed of marble quarried from Westchester County, the interior features a non-Greek rotunda. It is the site, however, rather than the building, that carries the historical import: George Washington took his oath of office in front of this structure's predecessor, Manhattan's city hall (which was called Federal Hall).

From Federal Hall to Federal Hall, the cycle has been completed.

Park Avenue Hotel

Palm Garden, Park Avenue Hotel, N. Y. City

The Park Avenue Hotel's Palm Garden—and the rest of the hotel as well—were luxurious reflections of the street on which it sat. Of late, even automobiles are named in honor of this slice of Manhattan real estate, while television commercials extol its exclusivity.

And why not? Along its wide boulevard are—or have been—landmarks to both gentility and architectural modernity. Fashionable apartment houses and clubs compete with the likes of the Seagram Building, the Lever House with its green-tinted glass, the General Electric Building, and St. Bartholomew's Church.

And for many decades, residing in pretension and splendor between Forty-ninth and Fiftieth streets, the yet world-famous Waldorf-Astoria Hotel.

35

The Hippodrome

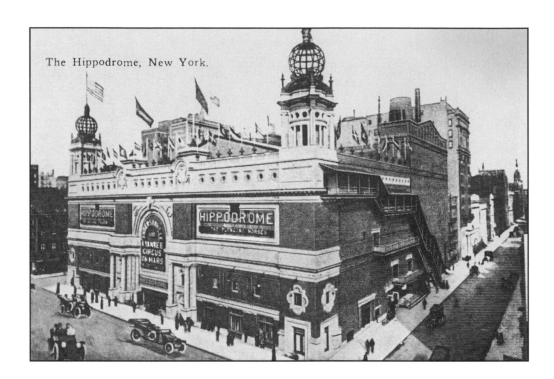

The Hippodrome, New York.

A bit of Coney Island in midtown Manhattan, the Hippodrome was owned and operated by—who else?—showman P. T. Barnum. The site itself has a somewhat checkered past, which makes for some interesting investigation.

The Vanderbilts' New York and Harlem Depot (Twenty-sixth Street and Madison Avenue) was an earlier occupant of the location before they abandoned it. Barnum converted it to Gilmore's Garden and, later, the Hippodrome. The crowds who came were drawn by spectacles; a few of these, like evangelists Dwight L. Moody and Ira Sankey's revival meet-

ings, were legitimate and meritorious. Other events, such as bare-knuckled boxing, horse shows, and burlesque acts of various sorts, amounted to little more than tasteless pandering (note the wording on this card: "Yankee Circus on Mars").

Refinanced (by Barnum and J. P. Morgan), restructured, and renamed Madison Square Garden in 1879, it underwent yet another face lift in 1892 when architect Sanford White set up residence on its roof garden. There, in 1906, his life ended in tragedy at the hands of Henry Thaw, husband of actress Evelyn Nesbit, White's former mistress.

Fordham Road

FORDHAM ROAD, FORDHAM, N.Y.C.

When Fordham Road is mentioned, two images immediately spring to mind: Fordham University and the Bronx. Both are significant parts of New York itself.

Where is the world-famous Bronx Zoo? Where is Yankee Stadium? Where is the renowned Bronx Museum of the Arts? Where is the Barton-Pell Mansion? Where is the Hall of Fame for Great Americans, with its unmatched sculpture?

These Bronx institutions, like the Borough itself, each have unique beginnings. Each have much to commend them. Take Fordham University, for instance. Its founder (John Hughes) became New York's first Catholic archbishop, while its first president (John McClosky) went even further, becoming America's first cardinal. The former Jesuit institution, begun in 1846, was renamed Fordham University in 1905. Its eighty-plus-acre campus has buildings ranging in style from Greek Revival to Collegiate Gothic to Gothic Revival. It is rumored that nearby resident Edgar Allan Poe wrote his poem "The Bells" in deference to Fordham's university church bell (now called "Old Edgar"). There is also the tale that James Fenimore Cooper's *The Spy* was written with this setting, still maintaining a somewhat rustic appearance, very much in mind.

A trip down Fordham Road, or anywhere else in the area, reveals more than one something about the Bronx. It tells the visitor that this Bronx, this home of the rich and poor, this intensely, ethnically diverse community, this site of museums and educational institutions, is at once both unique and all-American. It is Old World and new architecture. It is professional and laborer. It is artisan and mechanic. It is Fordham Road and Fordham University.

It is for real.

Essex Street

Copyright 1905 by the Rotograph Co.

A 170a. Essex Street, N. Y. City.

How is this for a busy street? Do I owe you a letter? Until July 25 my address will be care of Arthur L. Cook, 1703 Sterling Place, Brooklyn, N.Y. Shall be glad to hear from you. Edith Jones.

In at least one respect this circa-1910 scenic of Essex Street mirrored much of the rest of lower Manhattan in those days of the long ago: crowded, cramped, and always on the move.

The card itself says it all, with the simple handwritten question on the front: "How is this for a busy street?"

The same question could still be asked today, especially of the New Essex Street Market.

Metropolitan Life Insurance Building

Metropolitan Life Insurance Building, New York.

The seven-hundred-foot Metropolitan Life Insurance Tower was the world's tallest building when it was completed in 1909. It was—and is—also quite picturesque in the bargain. The four-faced clock (each face 26½ feet in diameter) has seven-hundred-pound hour hands and minute hands topping the scales at a half ton each. The clock dials are thus three stories high; the clock chimes a measure from Handel every fifteen minutes from seven A.M. until ten at night (the largest of the four chimes weighs a whopping seven thousand pounds).

A skywalk connects the tower to Met Life's North Building. Numerous other structures of prominence, including the Madison Avenue Presbyterian Church, had sat on the site previously, giving the North Building something of an illustrious prehistory. More newsworthy, if less tasteful, was an incident that took place in the New York Life Insurance Building only one block removed from the Met. There, on the New York Roof Garden (the previous Madison Square) in 1906, the eminent architect Sanford White was shot to death by a jealous husband.

The Met Life Building is now part of a complex annexed by Everett Waid and Harvey Corbet's building in 1933 and remodeled in 1961–62 by Lloyd Morgan, who stripped off much of the ornamentation. The North Building remains sufficiently appealing to have attracted the interests of movie moguls, who used it as a backdrop for several films.

Wanamaker's Department Store

Wanamaker's Department Store, New York.

Few men have made as big a name for themselves in one town as John Wanamaker did in two. In this case success bred success as Wanamaker's commercial venture in Philadelphia propelled him to New York, where he assumed he could do equally as well. He was correct, at least for several decades.

Rather than carving out a piece of real estate for himself, Wanamaker wisely chose to capitalize on an already proved name: He purchased the enterprises of A. T. Stewart, who had built America's premier department store behemoth, thus appropriating both Stewart's good name and his clientele. Unsatiated, Wanamaker erected the annex seen here, larger even than Stewart's original store, a monument to giantism and to the public's shopping thirst.

Radio City Music Hall

Since its opening in December of 1932, its popularity has been so great that a trip to New York was not considered to have been either thorough or enjoyable unless Radio City was on the itinerary. Small wonder: The Hall's opulence, its entertainment variety, and its special-event occurrences, along with the timeless appeal of its precision-dancing Rockettes (who started in St. Louis in 1925), render it quintessential New York at New York's quintessential best. Radio City is New York strutting its considerable stuff.

A travelogue of the 1940s describes the interior of Radio City in glowing terms: "This 6,200 seat vision of modernity and romanticism includes a sixty-foot high foyer overlooking a magnificent grand stairway. Everywhere one looks the appeal of gold is to be encountered: gold wall mirrors majestic in height, oil paintings in both massive and delicate Midas-gold frames, even a ceiling decorated in gold leaf. Sculptures of exquisite delineation are to be seen throughout, and the paintings of famous artists enliven or work to sombering effect at various locations within the majestic interior. Hidden lights suffuse the majestic modern auditorium. . . ."

Other facts spring to mind: The four-hundred-thousand-dollar stage consisted of three seventy-foot sections that were capable of being raised to fourteen feet above stage level. The Hall contained the world's largest screen (seventy feet by forty feet) and the world's largest theater orchestra. Two ton chandeliers and a gigantic Wurlitzer organ were but two more complements to the grandness everywhere abounding. The building itself is still the largest indoor theater in the world. From classic movies and highbrow entertainment to the electricity of Jerry Garcia and the Grateful Dead, Radio City Music Hall has served as a beacon to draw entertainer and patron alike to its environs.

It does still.

41

In Chinatown

8984 IN CHINATOWN, NEW YORK.

Few places in Manhattan are described in as varying a manner as Chinatown. "Exotic," "crowded," "heavenly" (usually said in reference to the cuisine) are but three descriptions, among many others. All are accurate, to one degree or another.

Before the arrival of the Chinese, which occurred in the period shortly before the Civil War, Chinatown was peopled largely by middle-class and wealthy families. The seven-year time frame from 1875 to 1882 (the year of the Chinese Exclusion Act) witnessed the greatest migration to the area when Asians became the local residents.

For decades the brotherhood known as the Tongs ruled Chinatown with rigid discipline, sometimes fighting one another in territorial power disputes. Although events of this nature have long been a thing of the past, legends and stories linger, adding luster to beliefs about Asian trickery and inscrutability.

Mulberry Street

2041 — Mulber... ...ew York.

Souvenir Post Card Co., New York and Berlin.

Mulberry and Mott streets are main thoroughfares that traverse both Little Italy and Chinatown in Manhattan. During the latter part of the nineteenth century, Mulberry Bend (on Mulberry Street between Bayard and Park) was one of the most run-down areas in Manhattan, or anywhere else in New York, for that matter. After criticism by social reformer Jacob Riis, Mulberry Bend was torn down and replaced by Columbus Park in 1892.

The postcard scene shown here is clearly more Italian than Asian, though street vendors who sold vegetables and fresh fruit were fixtures in both locales.

Pell Street

Pell Street, New York

Though a rather short street, hemmed in on the east by the Bowery and on the west by the curvature of Mott Street, Pell is one of the Chinatown's most traveled venues. Many of the vegetables served in the restaurants on Pell were actually grown on Long Island, but the preparation and taste were pure Chinese. In some places this is still the case, while other establishments offer a mixture of Thai and Vietnamese cuisine.

Chop suey is reported to have come into existence in Chicago in 1896 during the visit of Li Hung Chang, a renowned "ambassador of goodwill." The literal translation ("hodgepodge") is an appropriate one. New York's Chinatown has its own concoctions, universally praised. It is said that a trip to Chinatown is an opportunity to savor the best in Chinese cuisine this side of Canton. If that trip were made in the early years of the twentieth century, and if the traveler happened to stumble into the Old Chatham Club, he or she would have had a special treat. For on that staff was a young singing waiter named Israel Baline, who wisely changed his handle to a name beloved by all Americans: Irving Berlin.

Park Row

Park Row, New York.

The multifaceted history of New York City is writ large in almost every square foot of space in all five boroughs. Some locations and some streets, however, are clearly more historically significant than others. Park Row is one of these.

Adjoining the east side of City Hall Park in lower Manhattan, Park Row was previously known as Newspaper Row. Between the 1860s and into the second decade of the twentieth century, almost two dozen daily newspapers plied their trades here, each wanting to increase circulation at the others' expense. William Randolph Hearst and Joseph Pulitzer were the two most notorious of the warring print magnates, but there were many others. What most of them shared was print geared toward sensationalism, with, now and again, an honest attempt at muckraking to uncover corporate or political chicanery. This, in turn, led to charges of "yellow journalism" by those being vilified.

Such charges did not matter to these owners and editors, but circulation numbers did, so they kept hammering away to appease a growing public appetite for scandal. The other side of the coin was to be found in the fact that the era was certainly an interesting one for readers of newspapers and other popular periodicals. It was a time when they could peruse the writings of O. Henry and Richard Harding Davis while these authors espoused their social views in print, often wrapped in story form; a time when the merits of Social Darwinism, with its justification for the sometimes unscrupulous practices of robber barons, could be examined; a time when Upton Sinclair could write *The Jungle,* exposing the corrupt practices of the meatpacking industry, which surprised and energized then president Theodore Roosevelt into supporting passage of pure food and drug laws.

It was, in short, a time when seemingly everyone had an agenda to forward. And, on Park Row at least, a print media in which to promote it.

RCA Building

No name in modern times is more readily identified with New York City than that of John David Rockefeller. The images that name conjures are those of money, power, and prestige. Nowhere is this imagery more clearly seen—or felt, since a tour of the place is as much a inner or emotional experience as it is an empirical, sight-filled one—than at Rockefeller Center.

The Center was designed, and building on it begun, during the 1920s. That was the beginning only. At that time Rockefeller Center was bounded by Fifth and Sixth avenues and West Forty-eighth and Fifty-first streets. It then covered twelve acres. It now extends to Seventh Avenue and Fifty-second Street, a twenty-two-acre expansion.

The RCA Building, sometimes referred to as "the Slab," for self-evident reason, is shown here. It was placed at the Center's center. Seventy floors high, it was for many years the largest office building in the world. Currently it is home to the headquarters of the NBC television network, including a studio where the popular *Today* program has been broadcast since its inception in 1952.

Main Gate, Fort Hamilton

MAIN GATE, FORT HAMILTON, BROOKLYN, N.Y.

Though it is the third-oldest continuously garrisoned federal post in the United States, Fort Hamilton never had reason to assume an active military posture, nor was a single shot ever fired in battle from it. Built in 1831, its vertical-walled masonry rendered it obsolete for defense purposes as early as the Civil War period.

From that time it has been used first as a barracks, later as a post stockade, and lastly, beginning in 1938, as an officers' club. Throughout, it maintained a military appearance, with its granite blocks, wooden structures, and a main gate with the obligatory standing guard.

The main fort has been converted to a private club, but much of the original architecture is incorporated in the Harbor Defense Museum of New York City. It is well worth a drive down Fort Hamilton Parkway to see and tour it.

Originally the fort was called The Narrows, but its name was later changed in honor of Alexander Hamilton. As late as the 1940s Fort Hamilton was the headquarters of the First Division, the Fifth Coast Artillery, detachments of the Quartermaster Corps, and the Signal Corps, with about a thousand officers and men within 155 acres of enclosed ground.

Sunken Gardens, RCA Building

125:—SUNKEN GARDENS AND FOUNTAIN FRONT OF R. C. A. BUILDING, NEW YORK.

1020

Part of the glitz and not a little of the glamour of New York City is embodied by Rockefeller Center. The RCA Building is an excellent illustration of this majesty on display. Statuary such as the gold-leaf water-surrounded Prometheus, seen here, embolden and highlight this entrance to the building. Even more striking is the Zeus sculpture above the entrance doors. Created in limestone, it was cast in glass by the same artist (Lee Lawrie) who sculpted the giant Atlas on Fifth Avenue.

Inside the building are murals, panels, and paintings enough to satiate even the most zealous of connoisseurs. Barry Faulkner's glass mosaic, created with the use of over a million pieces of glass in more than two hundred shades of color, decorates the Sixth Avenue entrance.

Though the RCA Building became the GE Building when it was purchased by that latter corporation in 1986, the glamour, with even more compelling additions, has been retained.

The twenty-one high-rise office buildings with the almost three dozen restaurants, several television studios, at least one museum, and several convention halls that make up Rockefeller Center itself are decidedly impressive. Just what one would expect from a city with New York's reputation.

American Museum of Natural History

American Museum of Natural History, New York.

One measure of a city's cultural richness and diversity is to be found in its museums of science, history, and art. In this respect New York City has much to commend it, and of which to be proud.

The massive American Museum of Natural History, located at Central Park West, is but one example of that pride manifesting itself. Incorporated in 1889, the museum eventually became a research laboratory, a publishing house for scientific manuscripts, a sponsor of exploration, and a center for advanced study. Exhibits have been—and are—inclusive, with such fields of inquiry as anthropology (with its many sub areas of study), paleontology, geography, geology, biology, ethnology, and phenomena of all types, both naturally occurring and esoteric, being on display.

It would be difficult to overestimate the variety offered by the 36 million items to be seen: Flora and fauna, both living and deceased; skeletal remains and skeletal reconstructions; rock and mineral displays; slide presentations; lectures by experts in various fields of concentration; even drama and dance for both educational and entertainment purposes. Anyone interested in former president Theodore Roosevelt, especially his exploits and interest in hunting and big game, will be immeasurably pleased by the uniformed statue of him on horseback and the sound of his "voice" explaining some of the displays.

The Romanesque structure is the largest science museum in the world, four blocks long. Its legacy being to explain both the natural world and people's place in it, it succeeds admirably in this endeavor.

American Museum of Natural History

50

A sprawling (Seventy-seventh to Eighty-first streets and Central Park West) mesh of "wings" representing various architectural styles, the American Museum of Natural History is as much worth a look-see as are the exhibits inside the buildings.

Begun in 1874 by noted architects Calvert Vaux and Jacob Wrey Mould, the original plans called for a Victorian Gothic building. This early section is a five-story structure of red brick with brownstone trim. It may be viewed only from Columbus Avenue. The more well-known Romanesque Revival section on West Seventy-seventh, whose construction was not completed until 1899, was the work of Cleveland Cady. By that time he had added east and west ranges. The pink Vermont granite was a nice touch, softening and personalizing the basic features, which included corner towers, turrets, and dormers. The seven-bay arcaded porch and magnificent sweeping staircase are master strokes.

The accolades for further additions are not quite so effusive. Among them the most interesting architec-turally is the Roosevelt Memorial Hall and its interior. Trowbridge and Livingstone designed the north wing of the hall. John Russell Pope is responsible for the interior. The building is of gray granite; a broad beaux-arts entrance is complemented by four Ionic columns on sculpted plinths (animal representations), a figure-filled cornice (Lewis and Clark, John James Audubon, and Daniel Boone), and a sculpture of an equestrian Theodore Roosevelt in the company of an American Indian and an African tribesman.

The interior is more daunting still—or perhaps "intimidating" is a better word. The barrel-vaulted ceiling seems to reach to heaven in height, while the Corinthian columns inside the doors and to the sides are awe inspiring, both by reason of their height, and because they are constructed of the very sightly Alcanti and Verona marbles on Botticini bases. The statuary gracing the floors, and the murals displaying scenes of Roosevelt's life, attempt to decorate what is sometimes referred to as a sterile environment.

Police Headquarters

Police Headquarters,
Centre and Broome Sts., New York.
COPYRIGHT, 1910, BY IRVING UNDERHILL, N.Y.

The formidable, yet tasteful, exterior of New York City's former Police Headquarters Building in Manhattan is a pleasant reminder of what civic pride is presumably all about. Built between the years 1905–9, the structure came into being through the efforts and expertise of architects Francis Hoppin and Terence Koen. Theirs was no easy task, as the site selected for the station, at Centre and Broome streets, was so configured as to accept an elongated or wedge-shaped building.

This is what Hoppin and Koen supplied in the form of a flowing structure with semiclassical styling. The facade is not unlike English baroque, but the Corinthian columns are Greek architecture at its daunting best. The pediment features the female figure of Manhattan; the other four boroughs are represented as maidens. The entrance has two statues, while the picturesque tower has a column drum and a column lantern accompanying the high dome.

Though one hesitates to use the word "elegant" in re-

ferring to a police station, the term might fairly be said to apply to certain exterior aspects of the building, including its symmetrical appearance. As with the building, so with the officers themselves. The star-shaped copper badge (hence the term "cop") was still in evidence at this juncture in New York history.

But changes were on the way. By and large a taciturn, serious group, the police refused at first to wear the blue uniforms that were foisted upon them, thinking such attire had too much of a domestic flavor to it. Such men must have furnished visitors a more ambiguous perspective than the mere sight of the building, devoid of officers, might have done.

Too solid and historical a structure to destroy (besides, how would the city have made efficient use of the odd-shaped area?), it was converted into fifty-five fashionable condominiums in 1987. The police department had vacated the building in 1973.

East Side Free Baths

148a. "Ladies' Day" at the East Side Free Baths, N. Y. City.

New York was not the only city in America to offer free bathing facilities to its citizenry, but Gotham certainly built them on a grander scale. Indeed, it is doubtful if any city since ancient Rome could rival New York in this regard.

Between 1902 and 1915 thirteen public baths were built for the then astronomical sum of $2 million. Some possessed real architectural splendor; others were somewhat less magnificent structures: None of them were commonplace, constructed as they were along classical lines.

The bathhouse on East Twenty-Third Street is an example worthy of mention. Housing both recreational and bathing facilities, it featured 155 shower stalls with separate waiting rooms and showers for men and women. Both sexes had access to the huge pool, the sight of which was seen as a gift to poorer folk who lived in their near-indigent neighborhoods with, at best, a rudimentary sanitation system.

The columned fountained Twenty-third Street facility, with its prominently displayed water wings, realized a fate preferable to that of most other bathhouses: While many of them were being torn down to accommodate urban renewal plans, Twenty-third Street's minimonument serves as a recreation and community center.

East Side

44117   Monday morning on the East Side,
New York

Among the things for which Manhattan's Lower East Side is known are shipping and immigration. Many of these immigrants moved from the area after achieving some measure of economic success. Others have stayed from one generation to the next, flooding that portion of the Lower East Side below Chinatown with second-hand shops, flea markets, and street booths.

Ethnically diverse, the area is sociologically instructive. For the visitor it represents a bargain-filled, sometimes exciting, adventure.

Bedford Avenue, Brooklyn

Bedford Avenue, Brooklyn, N.Y.

Bedford Avenue, which runs from an area just south of Queens and across the Brooklyn–Queens Expressway to Sheepshead Bay, is one of Brooklyn's most well-known thoroughfares. Residing along its pavement, immediately north of Prospect Park, is the Muse Community Museum, while the Brooklyn Center for the Performing Arts and Brooklyn College's Walt Whitman auditorium are within parking and walking distance. Like much of the rest of Brooklyn, parts of Bedford Avenue are ethnic and racial in composition, maintaining identities of which the residents are proud.

This pre-1920 winter view reflects another Bedford Avenue, one that is quieter, if not happier—a time when vehicular traffic was sparse and familiar structures dotted the landscape.

Twenty-third Street

12134 23RD STREET. NEW YORK.

Much like Times Square was to become later, Twenty-third Street in the latter part of the nineteenth century was one of New York's premier entertainment locations. This was especially the case for that section of Twenty-third that crossed the Chelsea neighborhood in midwestern Manhattan. The Twenty-third Street theater was to become a movie house at a later date; but earlier on its playhouse stage and vaudeville background saw the small and great (including the "Jersey Lily" herself, Lily Langtry) both performing and in attendance.

The RKO Theatre, built in 1868 for a million dollars, was another Twenty-third Street landmark. Alternately known as Pike's Opera House (later changed to Grand Opera House), its partner owners were the famous millionaire Jay Gould and James Fisk, a newsmaker in his own right. When Gould and Fisk's attempt to corner the gold market failed, resulting in the Black Friday panic of 1869, "Diamond Jim" barricaded himself in the Opera House. Fisk was later shot in a quarrel with another man, which involved his girlfriend, Josie Mansfield. Obviously, Manhattan had some dime-novel material of its own going on.

In another area of Chelsea (on Twenty-sixth Street), Mary Pickford's first motion pictures were made on the top floors of an old armory building. In fact, several early cinema companies had studios in Chelsea, not a few of them burned to the ground on a more-or-less routine basis. Theft among these companies was rife, but this did not deter them, as they continued making their one- and two-reelers, perfecting their nascent craft. Eventually the wisest deserted New York altogether, finally arriving in the more wide-open and warmer clime of southern California.

Twenty-third Street Shopping

Midway between Central Park's southern extremity and Manhattan's toe, Twenty-third Street is an east-west thoroughfare between the Hudson and East rivers. Its most well-known section is the terminus where it crosses Broadway and Fifth Avenue, forming the southern end of Madison Park.

As can be observed on this postcard scenic, Twenty-third was heavily trafficked both by pedestrians and by various types of mechanical and motor-driven transport.

YMCA, Brooklyn

Young Mens Christian Ass'n., Sand Street, Brooklyn, N. Y.

It is interesting to note how so many of America's YMCAs built during the latter-nineteenth and early-twentieth centuries resembled one another architecturally—and also how few of the buildings that replaced them from the midtwentieth century forward have improved on the appearance of these earlier structures.

Red brick, limestone, or sandstone often formed the basis of these buildings' facades; and strict propriety of behavior formed the demeanor of the men who lived or sought Christian entertainment or exercise within their walls.

Most of these buildings have either been converted for other uses or demolished altogether. All too often the guiding principles of the YMCA were also victims to conversion or demolition, "the Y" having become just another anonymous building in just another anonymous city.

Clearly, the chain-store mentality at work.

Swedish Lutheran Church

SWEDISH LUTHERAN GUSTAF ADOLPHUS CHURCH, 22ND ST., NEAR 3RD AVE., NEW YORK.

This early twentieth-century view of the Swedish Lutheran Gustaf Adolphus Church indicates that Scandinavians existed in sufficient numbers in Manhattan by that time to justify the erection of such an impressive structure.

Actually, the Swedes had been coming to American shores since colonial times, adding to the cultural mixture not only in New York but also in other areas along the Eastern Seaboard, and into the American hinterland as well. Indeed, Swedish characterizations in the popular media for the better part of the last two centuries illustrate how thoroughly they have achieved acceptance and recognition within American society.

New York—Astor House

Although the Waldorf-Astoria, with its restored art-deco elegance, may be considered the architectural crown jewel of the Astor family's holdings, it was not their first offering in the hotel business. In fact, it was not even their second, that distinction going to the 1893 Waldorf-Astoria that preceded the current one (which was itself replaced in 1931 by the monumental Empire State Building).

The "first" title belongs to the Astor House, which John Jacob Astor built in 1836. Six stories in height and containing three-hundred rooms, the lower-Broadway fixture was a model of modernism. It featured public room, interior plumbing—even seventeen bathrooms —and was considered one of Manhattan's brightest ornaments.

Astor House

This view of the Astor House, identical to the previous one, is clearly of poorer visual quality. This is not uncommon for later photographic reproductions of the period, as the image itself would often become dull and indistinct with improper handling and storage. The fact that the image was reproduced at a later date highlights the early-twentieth-century interest generated both by this hotel, and, more generally, by anything to which the name "Astor" was attached.

Of note is the fact that the original Waldorf-Astoria was already into its second decade of existence when this postcard was produced.

Hester Street, New York

Hester Street, New York.

Though this row of multistoried buildings in a city of lesser size than New York might indicate economic prosperity, in The Big Apple this scenic speaks to the lower end of the socioeconomic ladder.

Hester Street in lower Manhattan, both at the turn of the century when this postcard was produced and also at present, is an avenue for overt human activity that includes both adults and children. Generations of immigrants worked, played, and transacted business on Hester, all wanting to establish themselves in the New World and create a better life than what they had known in their homeland.

For the children, often oblivious to their urban squalor, each day presented new opportunities for exploration, their combined antics creating a circus atmosphere amid the commerce.

Center, Shopping District

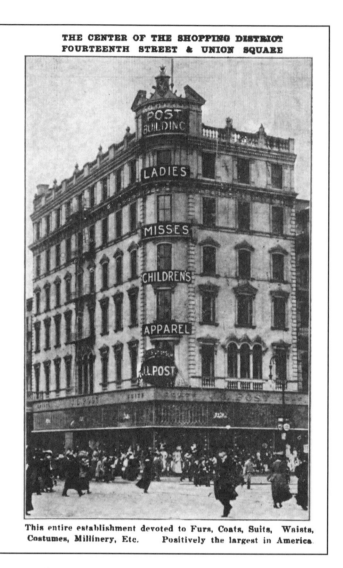

THE CENTER OF THE SHOPPING DISTRICT
FOURTEENTH STREET & UNION SQUARE

POST BUILDING

LADIES

MISSES

CHILDRENS

APPAREL

L POST

This entire establishment devoted to Furs, Coats, Suits, Waists, Costumes, Millinery, Etc.   Positively the largest in America.

It is not surprising that a city as actively occupied with the business of business as Manhattan obviously is would boast several sections of town that would lay claim to being *the* premier shopping area.

Thirty-fourth Street was clearly considered one of the top shopping arenas in town for most of this century. It is equally clear that both Times Square and the Post Building, shown here, were not lagging in the ability to attract customers to their own locales.

The Little Church around the Corner

4A-H1084

Officially named the Church of the Configuration, this Gothic-style structure has been, among other things, a popular wedding chapel for much of the twentieth century. Completed in 1861 from the design of an unknown architect, the Little Church around the Corner is located at 1 East Twenty-ninth Street in Manhattan. A lych-gate offers entrance to the grounds, which include a beautiful garden.

A much-loved institution.

Hawaiian Room, Hotel Lexington

The Famous *Hawaiian Room · Hotel Lexington* New York

In the year 1959 it could truthfully be said (and was) that the face of one man had been seen by more people than any other face since the beginning of time. That face belonged to Arthur Godfrey, and the place where his familiar mien could be viewed, his trusty ukulele always at the ready, was the Hawaiian Room of New York's famous Lexington Hotel.

Mixing architectural and decorational styles, this Manhattan landmark was completed in 1929 as part of the American Hotel Corporation. Its location on Lexington Avenue at East Forty-eighth Street proved fortuitous.

Though the avenue had been in economic decline for some time previously, it began to prosper shortly before the hotel's erection. Like the Waldorf-Astoria a few blocks away (built two years later in 1931), the Lexington combined elegant decor and art-deco splendor.

The Normanesque terra-cotta figures highlighting the Lexington Avenue entrance are reminiscent of those seen on the Notre Dame. Rows of winged lions, also of terra-cotta, decorate the hotel's facade, while the interior vaulted ceiling displays rows of dragons, griffins, and flowers.

Hotel Lexington

Though the Hawaiian and Revere rooms are no longer part of the Lexington's decor, there is yet much of the original hotel that remains.

This is as it should be, given that the building's architects, Schultze and Weaver, were men of no small reputation, being responsible for the Biltmores in Miami and Los Angeles, as well as for New York's Park Lane, Sherry Netherland, and the art-deco towers of the Waldorf-Astoria.

Inside the Lexington's entranceway, eighteen allegorical figures representing the Sciences, Art, and Progress protrude from above, a half dozen on each side. The marble-floored lobby is impressively illuminated by a giant three-tier chandelier.

And more: Polished brass doors on the elevators are decorated with birds and stylized dragon lizards; a large oriental rug in gorgeous shades of dark purple and pink rust both graces and dominates the lobby floor; historic, colorful prints of nineteenth-century New York are in evidence; a "Denim and Diamonds" nightclub showcasing country-western dance and music is on the premises; and J. Sung Dynasty's gourmet Chinese restaurant provides the flavor of the old Hawaiian Room.

Clearly, the Lexington Hotel now is what it then was: seven-hundred rooms and twenty-seven floors of comfort, delight, and artistry.

CHAPTER 3

Midtown New York Skyline

183:—MIDTOWN NEW YORK SKYLINE SHOWING WELFARE ISLAND, NEW YORK.

44251

One would need to study the history of the ancient world or that of modern Russia to find locations that have undergone as many name changes as the little piece of water-surrounded real estate pictured in this foreground.

The first name we are aware of is that of Minna-hanonck, a linguistic mouthful for even the American Indians who so designated it. When Governor Van Twiller purchased the Island in 1637 (he also bought Randall's, Ward's, and Governor's islands), it was used as a pasture for swine, thus the name Varcken—or Hog—came into popular use. The English mispronounced it until at length it came to be called Perkins Island by them. Robert Blackwell, who was married to the stepdaughter of another of the Island's owners, gave the Island the name it maintained, Blackwell's Island, until 1921.

In 1828 the city of New York had purchased the Island for $32,500 and commenced the building of hospitals, prisons, and other social institutions on it, another sidelight to its fascinating history. In 1921 the name was changed to Welfare Island by the city's board of alderman.

The final name change occurred in the 1970s, when it was designated Roosevelt Island in honor of the Depression-era president Franklin Delano Roosevelt. It has since been given over primarily to housing (with a few buildings, park areas, promenades, and the like scattered about), the thought being to create a new city on the East River.

Skyscrapers in Midtown Manhattan

Skyscrapers in Mid-town Manhattan, New York City 112

K 1955

Ewing Galloway Photo

No other skyline in the world resembles that of Manhattan. Then again, no other city has Manhattan's distinctive buildings. Somehow the Empire State and Chrysler buildings (among others) would seem inappropriate anywhere but here.

Stranger still is the fact that most out-of-towners who recognize this vignette would refer to it as belonging not to Manhattan, but to New York City. For them Manhattan *is* New York, giving the city two names, while Brooklyn, Queens, and the Bronx are just that:

Brooklyn, Queens, and the Bronx. Perhaps even more incomprehensible is the mind-set of millions of Americans who, if they heard the name Staten Island, would think of a boat ride rather than a borough.

New York City obviously does not begin and end in Manhattan, though that island is usually what's being referred to when the city is mentioned. For the other boroughs that fact is a nonstarter, conversationally speaking. They cherish their separate identities and unique characters.

Brooklyn Bridge

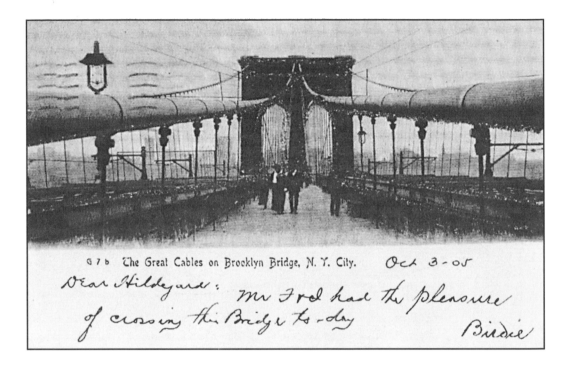

97b The Great Cables on Brooklyn Bridge, N. Y. City.   Oct 3-05

Dear Hildegard: Mr Frd had the pleasure of crossing this Bridge to-day

Birdie

Asked to identify a half-dozen New York City landmarks, most out-of-towners would include the Brooklyn Bridge in their enumeration. Many of them would probably include it even if the number of choices was limited to three, such is the bridge's hold on the American popular imagination. And how many times has some unsuspecting soul heard the question: "Want to buy the Brooklyn Bridge?"

Not surprisingly, the real bridge is every bit as impressive as its imaginary alter ego.

The bridge's story begins, as well it should, at the beginning. And that beginning existed in the mind of the bridge's creator, German immigrant John Augustus Roebling, not as a structure of steel and stone but as an idea—an idea that would grandly illuminate man's creative spirit. Roebling, a student of Hegelian philosophy and an inventor, had yet another advantage to his credit: Though he was an engineer, he was not an architect; thus his plans were not hindered by preconceived notions of form and function.

Where Roebling did learn much, beginning in 1837, was on his job with the canal system in Pennsylvania. While there, he designed an iron rope to replace the hemp rope then in use to pull the canal boats. He also developed new ideas for the usage of stronger cables in suspension bridges. This latter discovery was effectively tested through the designs of suspended aqueducts over the Allegheny River, and the construction of the Niagara Suspension Bridge and the Covington Bridge, which linked Ohio and Kentucky over the Ohio River in Cincinnati.

A good businessman in the bargain, Roebling established the lucrative Roebling Works in Trenton, New Jersey, which manufactured steel wire and cable.

He was now set for this crowning achievement, designing the world's longest (1,595 feet) suspension bridge between the behemoths of Manhattan and Brooklyn.

The year was 1867.

Approach to the Brooklyn Bridge

12498   APPROACH TO BROOKLYN BRIDGE, BROOKLYN, N. Y.

Originally the bridge was called the East River Bridge, because it would cross that body of water in order to unite Brooklyn and Manhattan. Its two most prominent features were the twin Gothic Revival towers needed to support the bridge's cables and stays. The four cables themselves are eleven inches in diameter, each one containing over thirty-five hundred miles of wire; the stays number in the hundreds, fanning out diagonally from the towers. An additional system of iron trusses was used to stabilize the structure during wind or rain storms. The main cables were anchored beneath the inclined roadways leading up to the bridge in giant vaults of granite and brick.

Roebling's greatest pride was in the towers (the Brooklyn tower was completed in May 1875, the Manhattan tower the following July). His prediction that they would be listed as national monuments was accurate: The Bridge was granted that status in 1964, eighty-one years after its completion in 1883.

As with Greek tragedy and life generally, the bridge's construction was not without unfortunate incident. More than twenty workers died during its erection, but not before John Roebling himself met misfortune. When his toes were accidentally crushed during the first weeks after the project began, Roebling foolishly refused conventional medical treatment. His own methodology for treating the ailment proved ineffective; he died shortly thereafter of lockjaw.

His son, Washington Roebling, succeeded his father, but himself suffered from a recurring case of bends throughout his life as a direct consequence of decompression from laboring on the bridge's subterranean foundations.

Thus was born the world's first all-steel suspension bridge—and a New York landmark of legendary proportions.

Ranked with the Crystal Palace in London (1851) and Paris's Eiffel Tower (1889) as one of the greatest architectural feats of the nineteenth century, the Brooklyn Bridge was every inch as much a challenge to construct as were they.

Roebling's proposed five lanes (two in the middle for cable trains, two outer lanes for horse-drawn carriages, and a fifth as a pedestrian strolling promenade) were both an innovation and a wise concession to all uses of the bridge that might have been envisioned. The five-cent toll for the train ride was another forethought whose purpose was to pay for building and maintenance of the bridge.

George Washington Bridge

76

14903

70

Fame, as the old saw would have it, is a fleeting thing. Even quite wonderful phenomena like bridges may see their celebrity slip away as they are replaced on the world stage by other phenomena thought to be more impressive by a humanity raised to believe that bigger is better and that more is somehow grander than less.

This fate could have befallen New York's George Washington Bridge. It could have, but it didn't. Built to a length of thirty-five hundred feet, making it the world's longest suspension bridge in 1931, it relinquished that honor a mere eight years later to that Golden Gate spectacle out there in San Francisco. Rather than accepting its presumed secondary status, the citizens of New York speak with pride about the George Washington, a pride that comes from knowing that one is talking about something important.

Indeed, it is the only New York City structure spanning the mighty Hudson and, as such, adds stature to the history and culture of Washington Heights. In tranquil grandeur, its features dominate the skyline.

Who said secondary?

Queensboro Bridge

Queensboro Bridge, New York.
COPYRIGHT 1909, BY IRVING UNDERHILL, N.Y.

This view of the Queensboro Bridge, which leads from East Fifty-ninth and Sixtieth streets in Manhattan across the East River to the Queens Plaza, illustrates its multifaceted, ponderous steel construction. Unlike New York's more delicate-appearing and artistically graceful suspension bridges, the Queensboro may seem clumsy by comparison.

One should not be misled. Indeed, the very complexity of this structure is worth studying. Nor is it less than impressive on the purely physical, substantive level. A great cantilevered presence costing $25 million to build, the Queensboro Bridge rests on six huge masonry piers. It is 7,636 feet long, its west span 1,182 feet, its clear height over channels 135 feet, the height of its Island tower 324 feet, its width 86 feet.

What these numbers do not tell, nor can they show, is the drama of the bridge's presence. Its silhouette is intricate either in the daytime, when one can see the various steel components clearly defined, or at night, when the partially lighted top creates its own luminescent delights.

Completed in 1909, Queensboro Bridge was the brainchild of architects Palmer and Hornbostel and the product of engineer Gustav Lindenthal.

And, of course, the labors of dozens of men, fifty of whom died during the Queensboro's construction.

Williamsburgh Bridge

WILLIAMSBURGH BRIDGE APPROACH, NEW YORK CITY.

Running from Delancy and Clinton streets in Manhattan to Brooklyn's Washington Plaza, the Williamsburgh Bridge was the second structure to cross the East River. Built in 1903 by engineer Leffert Buck, it is a steel suspension affair like the earlier-built Brooklyn Bridge. Unlike the Brooklyn Bridge, however, its support on the land side of the steel towers is by truss and pier rather than by pendant cable.

The bridge was named for the former town of Williamsburgh, which later united with greater Brooklyn.

Upper Broadway

From Battery Park in the south to Manhattan's Upper West Side, Broadway spans the entire length of the island. In fact, it runs farther north yet, into Yonkers and beyond.

Because of this its history is the most comprehensive and the most diverse of any street in New York. It has witnessed along its route poverty, wealth, architectural splendor, squalor, glamour, seediness, respectability, innovation, staidness, and revolution.

Consider that in its path is City Hall Park, Union Square Park, Madison Square Park, Herald Square, Times Square, Columbus Circle, Central Park, Riverside Drive, Morningside Park, Fort Tryon Park, and Inwood Hill Park.

If one word could describe Broadway, that word would be "energy." Or perhaps it would be "activity."

It would not be "dull." Or "boring."

Upper Broadway

Upper Broadway, New-York.

The liveliness of Broadway applies to both ends of it, and to its middle. Battery Park in the south was—and is—a recreational "class equalizer." Lower Broadway also contained fashionable neighborhoods and notable church structures, as well as historic City Hall Park, still an optical delight.

Upper Broadway, for the better part of the twentieth century, has been known as the setting for Times Square (with its combination of sultriness and legitimate theater), and for the Upper West Side generally which includes park enclaves, historic drives, pastoral settings, and picturesque views of the Hudson River.

Montauk Club

MONTAUK CLUB, Brooklyn, N. Y.
ILLUSTRATED POST CARD CO., N. Y.

2003

Located at the Grand Army Plaza in west central Brooklyn, the Montauk Club is one slice of that borough's nineteenth-century (1891) architectural history that has been preserved. Modeled on Venice's Ca'd'Oro, the Montauk is constructed of brick, terra-cotta, brownstone, and verdigris copper. Third- and fourth-story friezes depicting the Montauk Indians illustrate the building's origins. A Venetian Gothic palazzo, it is easily the most historically impressive structure in the area.

Twenty-Second Avenue Parkway, Bensonhurst

TWENTY-SECOND AVENUE PARKWAY, BENSONHURST, BROOKLYN, N. Y.

North of Coney Island and west of Sheepshead Bay, Bensonhurst is a predominantly Italian neighborhood (scenes from the movie *Saturday Night Fever* were shot here) with a long history.

Named for Charles Benson, whose farm occupied the site, this area of southwest Brooklyn includes Borough Park, much of which was owned by the prestigious Litchfield family and became, for a time, a wealthy Jewish enclave. The environment includes the former New Utrecht, a village originally settled in 1661, its surviving namesake (built in 1828) the New Utrecht Reformed Church on Eighteenth Avenue between Eighty-third and Eighty-fourth streets.

Bensonhurst today is characterized by Italian-style eateries and discount establishments. An interesting sidelight to the early illustration pictured here is the fact that the width of this parkway lets one know immediately that the view is of a borough with less cramped quarters than those of Manhattan.

Metropolitan Opera House

4694—
Metropolitan
Opera House
New York

An unimpressive, box-shaped building, this earlier home of the Metropolitan Opera House was anything but unimpressive inside. Initially, it had boxes on three tiers, but the third tier was so unpopular with ticket holders that it was eliminated. From that height the performers could hardly be seen; thus, the removal was a wise alteration.

The lower tier became the famous "diamond horseshoe," the glitter of jewels and fancy dress a match for the splendid interior decoration.

Located on Thirty-ninth and Broadway, "the Met" changed locations in 1966, moving farther up Broadway to Lincoln Center, where its glamour shone even more intensely in a glass-encased building housing brilliantly colored Chagall tapestries.

Pratt Institute, Brooklyn

Pratt Institute, Brooklyn. N. Y.

Seen here is the Pratt Institute's Main Building, the first structure (1885–87) to be built on the Clinton Hill site. Designed by Lamb and Rich, the six-story Romanesque Revival edifice features a central clock tower and eye-appealing corner towers.

The school itself was founded by oil magnate Charles Pratt, who had wisely joined his old empire with John D. Rockefeller's in 1874. Pratt, who considered himself a self-made man, founded the school with the purpose of training technicians and artisans. His school's objec-tive was to produce workers with mechanical and/or artistic ability rather than to graduate those with more intellectual passions. In this sense the Pratt Institute was a forerunner of the hundreds of trade schools that have flourished in America over the past century.

Among Pratt's graduates is Bill Gold (class of 1941), who is the most prolific movie-poster designer in the business.

Somewhere Charles Pratt must be beaming.

Pratt Institute Free Library

PRATT INSTITUTE FREE LIBRARY
BROOKLYN, NEW YORK

Although Charles Pratt was clearly more concerned with preparing students for manual training than with perfecting their academic skills, it is also the case that he considered reading to be a most worthwhile activity.

The Pratt Institute Free Library was built in 1896 after the design of William B. Tubby. It was the first free public library in Brooklyn, and a direct outgrowth of Pratt's theories abut self-help. His belief that man could better himself with training and access to broad learning put him in the forefront of those progressive thinkers willing to promote their ideas with their dollars.

This red-brick Renaissance Revival structure is three stories high and features round-arched windows on the second floor and a modillioned cornice supporting a balustraded parapet.

Other buildings on the campus include the South Hall (1889–91) and the Romanesque Revival Memorial Hall (1926–27).

Fifth Avenue, Waldorf-Astoria

3032 Fifth Avenue, Waldorf Astoria, N. Y. City.

Few hotels in all the world have the name recognition of the Waldorf-Astoria. The sound of that name conjures images of glamour and exclusivity. This is exactly what William Waldorf-Astor had in mind in 1893 when he built the thirteen-story Waldorf at Fifth Avenue and Thirty-fourth Street.

That, and the intent to keep his name, and his namesake, always fresh in the public's mind—a name and a namesake bespeaking opulence and splendor, the very epitome of class. The hotel was all of that, and became even more when it was joined by a corridor linking it to the seventeen-story Astoria Hotel erected on an adjacent site four years later. Henceforth the combined hostelries were called the Waldorf-Astoria.

For more than thirty years the hotel received through its exclusive doors the likes of kings, queens, prime ministers, and presidents—in addition to millionaires, movie stars, and other social elites.

Closed in 1929 to make way for the Empire State Building, the Waldorf-Astoria reopened two years later, even more magnificent than its predecessor. Stretching from Park Avenue to Lexington Avenue and occupying the entire block from Forty-ninth to Fiftieth streets, the new Waldorf-Astoria rose forty-two blocks above midtown Manhattan. Fifty red carpets were laid in front of the entrance to the twenty-two-hundred–room behemoth, which was immediately dubbed New York's first skyscraper hotel. President Herbert Hoover, later a resident of the Waldorf-Astoria, delivered a message of congratulations from his office in the White House as the doors were thrown open to the public for the first time.

How could one expect lesser treatment for a hotel that launched the careers of both Frank Sinatra and Diana Ross (in the Empire Room); a hotel that was the first hostelry in which a major motion picture was filmed (*Weekend at the Waldorf*); a hotel with song lyrics written about it ("You're a Waldorf Salad" from Cole Porter's *Anything Goes*); a hotel that introduced the concept of a retractable roof above its supper club; the only hotel to be the residence of three five-star generals (Dwight Eisenhower, Douglas MacArthur, and Omar Bradley)?

Like its earlier version shown here, the Waldorf-Astoria has been less concerned with its giantism than with its service and its impeccable quality.

Hors d'oeuvres, anyone?

Girl's High School, Brooklyn

Girl's High School, Brooklyn N.Y.

Lack of funding in small rural areas prevented the erection of unisex public educational institutions like the building seen here. Larger areas of population concentration, such as Brooklyn, considered separate institutions worth the additional expense, especially at the secondary level, in pre-1920 America.

Most such institutions built during the late-nineteenth and early-twentieth centuries have either been demolished or converted to other uses. Gothic and Romanesque were the prevailing architectural styles used for their erection. The atmosphere these schools generated was consistent with that of the classrooms inside, where decorum, rote methodology, and stern discipline were what one expected, and assuredly what one encountered.

New York Harbor

2015—New York Harbor

Oct 4, 96

Dear Tillie.
How would you like to pay $7.78 for my wash. Nellie

For all the talk about New York being a fashion center, an entertainment center, a banking center, and a publishing center, it is undeniably the case that the city is just as fundamentally a waterborne commerce center.

This has always been the reality; it will ever be the reality.

The 750-mile shoreline of the Port of New York accommodates activities ranging from freighter service to cargo shipping and receiving, to residential and recreational projects. The port provides docking space for more than 250 large ships at a time, handling in the neighborhood of twenty-thousand ship movements a year. Cargo tonnages are upwards of 50 billion tons per annum, the dollar value figure approaching $50 billion.

Almost four hundred thousand people a year book passage from one of the six piers located on the Hudson River between Forty-eighth and Fifty-second streets. The most well-known luxury liners in the world arrive and depart from these piers regularly, along with almost a hundred other steamships. Also increasing the dock's congestion are tens of thousands of trucks loading and unloading cargo for distribution in the United States and around the world.

Sailing Vessels at Dock

12051   SAILING VESSELS AT DOCK NEW YORK

By 1843 New York City was the second-largest port in the world, with sixty-three wharves on the East River and fifty on the Hudson. Only London exceeded it.

The Harbor's history has been a colorful one. A little-known fact is that a protest similar to that held in Boston a year earlier (1773) resulted in a band of New Yorkers dumping eighteen cases of tea into the Harbor.

The modern New York and New Jersey Port Authority oversees what can only be described as an empire.

The jurisdictional area exceeds fifteen hundred square miles (within a twenty-five-mile radius of the Statue of Liberty), in which it operates seven waterfront terminal areas. These include Manhattan's passenger-ship terminal, cargo piers in Brooklyn and Hoboken, and container ship terminals in Newark and Elizabeth, New Jersey.

Additionally, the Authority is responsible for the six tunnels and bridges connecting New York and New Jersey; airports, helioports, the Trans-Hudson (PATH) rail rapid transit system; and the colossal World Trade Center, which it built.

New York Public Library

New York Public Library, New York.

Every big city should have a big-city library, a repository and a dispenser of humankind's cultural heritage. New York City's public library system, with its ninety-two miles of books (or is it shelving?), is said to be second to none.

The main building's beginnings were auspicious. Combining the contents of both the Astor and Lennox libraries, along with a generous bequest from former New York governor Samuel Tilden, the New York facility was established in 1895. The cornerstone was not laid until 1902, however, and the building was not completed until 1911.

It was worth the wait. The architects, Carrere and Hastings, produced a structure both beautiful and utilitarian. Standing resplendently among a sea of modern architectural banality, the New York City Public Library is a testament to beaux-arts style and to American attention to functionality.

From the graceful Attic statuary representing allegorical figures relating to the spoken and written word, to the lions at the building's base, the entire enterprise is at once pleasing to the eye. The Corinthian columns, with their hydra-spouting acanthus-plant leaves, are an encounter with the beauty and the glory that was ancient Greece.

Its main reading room, a spacious, airy, high-stuccoed-ceiling affair, seats 768 readers in comfortable fashion.

This building is not beaux-arts at its New World best, nor is it New York at its most sublime: Rather, it is America at its old-time and all-time most magnificent.

One wishes it were the archetype of things to come.

Astor Library

Copyright 1905 by the Rotograph Co.
309   Astor Library, N. Y. City.

One of America's preeminent millionaires and entrepreneurs, John Jacob Astor fell a little short in the philanthropy department. At least, that is, while he was alive. Born to a German butcher, Astor had come to the United States in 1783 at the age of twenty. Known primarily as a fur-business baron, he was sufficiently shrewd enough to purchase real estate in Manhattan. All the rest—the hotels, houses, and speculative ventures—are part of the historical record.

So is the generous endowment that created the Astor Free Library. The story behind the generosity is less well-known. A teacher named James Green Cogswell worked on Astor for years before finally convincing him that a public library would serve as a more fitting testament to his memory than would another statue (a monument to Washington having been previously considered).

Cogswell's persistence and foresight paid dividends on two fronts. In the first instance, Astor's will left four hundred thousand dollars for the creation of the library, which was supplemented by a plot of land bequeathed to the city for placing it on. Books and later bequests by other members of the Astor clan brought the total donation to the million-dollar range.

Washington Irving was the library's first president, and the institution flourished, though insufficient lighting restricted its use initially to daylight hours.

Falling into disuse and disrepair when the city created its own public library system, the building came to serve two further functions. After briefly being utilized by the Hebrew Immigrant Aid Society, which had purchased the building in 1920, it later (1966) became the Public Theater. A redesigned interior made room for the theater, auditorium, and office. This last usage had the dual effect of reenergizing both the theatrical community, generally, and the area itself, specifically.

The books became part of the New York library system.

Broadway and Fifth Avenue

Broadway and Fifth Avenue looking north from 23rd St., New York.

This section of the intersection of Broadway and Fifth Avenue in Manhattan is the south end of Madison Square Park. Although some of the buildings are different now from what they were then, the geographical configuration is the same, illustrating why the intersection is not always easy to negotiate.

Another thing that remains constant is the congestion—both that of the traffic, and also that of the structures, close fitting and compactly aligned.

Tombs (City Prison)

TOMBS, (CITY PRISON) N.Y. CITY.

Cincinnati had its Work House, a forbidding mass of stone and mortar designed to break the spirit and exact retribution from social sinners. Portland, Oregon, had its Rocky Butte, a craggy affair reminiscent of the brooding darkness identified with medieval castles, its unpleasant task—one it performed well—to incarcerate and punish.

New York City had its own chamber of horrors, a ghastly edifice, both unsightly and unwelcoming, with a most likely nickname: the Tombs. Although the name is derived from an earlier building on the site that was used for the same purpose, it was also a suitable moniker for this structure.

Its rounded ends and witch's-hat roof bring to mind the inscription "Abandon hope, all ye who enter here." One further supposes that the classic "Ballad of Reading Gaol" could have been written to describe an establishment not unlike this one.

Used primarily as a holding location for men awaiting trial, the Tombs were finally vacated in 1939 upon completion of the new art-deco Criminal Courts Building and Prison. And not, as the cheap turn-of-the-century novels would say, a minute too soon.

Institute of Arts and Sciences

Institute of Arts and Sciences, Brooklyn, N. Y.

Easily one of the most impressive structures in Brooklyn is the Institute of Arts and Sciences, seen here on this early card. Begun in 1895 (or 1897—reports conflict), the neoclassical building was designed by the well-known architectural firm of McKim, Mead, and White. As a result of Works Progress Administration (WPA) work in 1934 and 1935, both the exterior and interior were altered (some think debased) with the removal of the outside stairway and the moving of the lobby downstairs to the basement. Both efforts were said to represent modernization and improvement.

Not tampered with is the rich ornamentation of the building's exterior. Standing with classical pride is the six-columned entrance portico flanked by heavy orna-mentation, including a steep pediment occupied by sculpted figures (thirty heroes from antiquity reside atop the cornice gracing each side of the portico).

Also of special mention are the two sculpted female figures of Manhattan and Brooklyn, executed by renowned sculptor Daniel Chester French. Originally situated at the Brooklyn end of the Manhattan Bridge, the statues were moved to the Institute in 1963 when their pedestals were destroyed by a road-project crew.

Fronds, rosettes, and scrolls embellish the pediment, while swags and lion's heads decorate the cornice behind it. Impressive by any standard.

Museum, Institute of Arts and Sciences

MUSEUM, INSTITUTE OF ART & SCIENCE, BROOKLYN, N. Y.

For this building, now known simply as the Brooklyn Museum, there is nothing simple about either its contents or its grounds. In addition to its well-publicized and appropriately well-received Egyptian and primitive art collections are numerous other items of merit.

These include artwork by European masters, outstanding paintings by American artists, an extensive print collection, and period rooms of note. Featured among this last is a suite of rooms from the John D. Rockefeller Mansion. Even more impressive is the architecturally intriguing Jan Martense Schenck House, a colonial residence (1675) that was dismantled and rebuilt inside the museum in 1952.

The Frieda Schiff Warburg Sculpture Garden (1966) at the building's rear showcases such pieces of New York history as column bases, a capital, and a sculpted figure from the highly regarded Pennsylvania Station; columns from the Bayard Building; and a lion's head from Coney Island's once magnificent, and ever-crowded, Steeplechase Park.

The New Fulton Fish Market

THE NEW FULTON FISH MARKET, NEW YORK CITY
Compliments of WARNER & PRANKARD, 22 Fulton Fish Market, N. Y.

Some traditions die hard; others refuse to die at all. The Fulton Fish Market fits securely and, it now seems, permanently into the latter category.

Established in 1821, Fulton's has operated continuously since that date, becoming, in the process, the largest fresh-fish market in America. It is nothing less than a South Street institution firmly embedded on the East River side of lower Manhattan. A fresh-fish receiving and distribution point for the city's supermarkets and restaurants, the Fulton Market has been described as the only location in Manhattan that is both smelly and popular.

Its proximity to the Fulton Market Building, with its exotic, esoteric groceries and bakeshops—and also to the famous South Street Seaport, with its multiple boutiques, restaurants, galleries, specialty shops, and cruise vessels—make these other areas primary sources of social and commercial activity.

Odds are, Fulton's will outlast them all.

Tradition clearly has a lasting place in New York.

Broad Street, near Wall

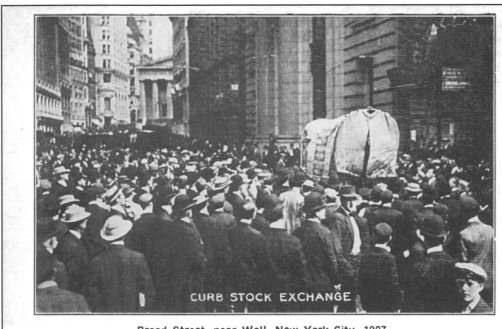

CURB STOCK EXCHANGE

Broad Street, near Wall, New York City, 1907.

There are streets in Manhattan with more eloquent architecture than that encountered on Wall or Broad. There are streets with a greater number of diversionary activities. And it is certain that there are more well-organized and tidier areas than Wall or Broad streets.

But what these avenues may lack in trendiness or cleanliness is more than compensated for by their pedigree and financial reputations.

But, first, a bit of logistical history is in order. Wall Street derives its name from the fortifications erected by Governor Peter Stuyvesant in 1653 at the direction of the Dutch West India Company. Engaged in a war with the British, they sought to insure New Amsterdam's security in the event of attack. Stuyvesant, however, chose a wiser course than that of encasing the entire colony as if it were a medieval fortress; instead,

he built a wall of oaken posts from the East River to the North River. The foundation consisted of a trench eleven feet wide and five feet deep. An entrance at Pearl Street (called the Watergate) provided both entry and egress from the land. The wall itself was constructed of posts thirteen feet in height and a little less than two feet in diameter. At sixteen-foot intervals larger posts were installed; split rails were nailed to them at both the top and the bottom. Drainage and protection were offered by the addition of a ditch three feet wide and two feet deep.

Wall Street was born. The crowds, seen here, would come later, along with a semiorganized type of mayhem.

So too would Trinity Church, Federal Hall, the Bank of New York, and numerous other financial institutions—in fact, the world's largest concentration of them.

Broad Street Curb Brokers

9270 BROAD STREET CURB BROKERS NEW YORK   COPYRIGHT, 1905, BY DETROIT PUBLISHING CO.

92

As this postcard, and the previous one, illustrate, Broad Street has more to commend it than its southwestern intersection with Wall to form the New York Stock Exchange. Home to numerous businesses, including those of a pecuniary nature, Broad, where it intersects with Pearl, is also the site of the historically significant Fraunces Tavern Museum. Composed of five buildings, including a restored eighteenth-century tavern where Washington bade farewell to his officers in 1783, the museum is a cherished landmark. Other structures attached to it house Americana from the eighteenth and nineteenth centuries, along with antique paper ephemera (manuscripts, prints, et al.), paintings, and rooms of period artifacts.

New York Stock Exchange

A 158   New York Stock Exchange, N. Y. City.

Fact: The address of the New York Stock Exchange is 8 Broad Street. Though Wall Street has the magic attached to its name, it is Broad that the post office recognizes as the home of the Stock Exchange.

The building itself is small compared to its towering neighbors. Yet there is clearly nothing small, but rather quite dominating, about the effect this one structure has on all of our lives. That was proved during the decade following the market's collapse in October of 1929, when the nation was plunged into its worst economic depression. More than being a set of daily numbers flashing on our television screens each evening, the stock market is America's economic lifeblood.

Architecturally speaking, the building itself is no less than impressive. Even if one did not know its function, one would be led to believe that this noble structure served some important use. A library, maybe, a government building of some sort, perhaps. Certainly not a supermarket, although in a very real sense the stock exchange can easily be compared to a store. Both handle staples and delights, necessities . . . and items of a more adventurous nature. (Rocky Road ice cream, or stocks in an emerging but still risky computer software firm—it's an interesting parallel.)

About the architecture: Six Corinthian columns and adjoining posts compete with the majestic pediment that is occupied by sculptures seemingly alive with activity. One sees Greek and Roman architectural models here, both at their finest. The Corinthian acanthus plant and the active, citizen-oriented statuary tell even the casual observer that business and civic pride can be made to appear as if they were cut from the same cloth, melding to become a whole from separate units.

Designed by architect George B. Post, this Greek Revival temple was, in fact, the second exchange building on Broad and Wall streets. The first, begun in 1863, was a four-story affair designed by John Kellum. Italianate in appearance, its marble face was pleasant enough to look upon, but the quarters proved insufficient; by the turn of the century the New York Stock Exchange Board sought larger accommodations. Adjacent land was purchased, and the Georgia-marbled, neoclassical facade was begun. Spending freely, Post built private consultation rooms, baths, a barbershop, even lounging rooms. Because the site was irregular, it was anchored on a two-story podium with a water table to compensate for the incline. Post's work was completed in 1903, but a later addition (1923) was executed by Trowbridge and Livingstone.

Unfortunately, New York's atmospheric conditions

caused the marble figures in the pediment (the work of J. Q. A. Ward and Paul Bartlett) to decompose. Titled, not surprisingly, *Integrity Protecting the Works of Man,* they had to be replaced by lead-covered copper reproductions, which have been sheathed in a coating made to resemble the stone originals.

A few more facts: Created at the close of the eighteenth century, the Stock Exchange had the primary function of handling the $80 million in U.S. bonds that had been issued in 1789 and 1790 to pay off debts incurred during the Revolutionary War. The Exchange took on a life of its own over the next century and has been flexing its not inconsiderable muscle ever since.

The invention of the stock ticker in 1867 created more than ticker-tape parades; the recording of stock sales on an ever-continuing paper and electronic basis keeps the public both informed and excited—or crestfallen— as the numbers tumble into view, then onto television screens, then into newsprint, then into history.

The frenetic pace of activity taking place on the trading-room floor under that eighty-foot ceiling is monitored throughout the world, a bellwether for financial markets across the globe. Over seventeen hundred of the world's largest companies issue nearly 80 billion shares of stock. The aggregate value of these exceeds $3 trillion.

The Ansonia

THE ANSONIA. The Largest Apartment Hotel in the World.
:: 2500 rooms :: Apartments and suites to suit every requirement.
NEW YORK, N. Y.

twenty-five hundred rooms, was reportedly the largest apartment hotel in the world. The genius behind it was William Earl Dodge Stokes, a developer of dozens of houses on the West Side in the 1880s. Stokes made the original drawings himself. In order to avoid costly fire-insurance premiums, he fireproofed the Ansonia by making three-foot-thick terra-cotta partitions. This offered the not-unwelcome additional benefit of soundproofing the rooms, a godsend for musicians and others who desired privacy. Among those to take advantage of this anonymity were Enrico Caruso, Igor Stravinsky, Yehudi Menuhin, Arturo Toscanini, and Lily Pons. Not to mention legendary showman Flo Ziegfeld and his wife, Billie Burke.

Not that the Ansonia didn't offer other inducements. Two swimming pools, four hundred fully equipped bathrooms, six hundred toilets and washbasins, and an orchestra that played on the rooftop on summer evenings. The roof also housed Stokes's garden and his animal collection, which included chickens, goats, ducks, and a pet bear. Eggs were sold to tenants for half price until a lawsuit discontinued this bit of free enterprise.

American in size (sixteen stories in height, covering a city block), but French in design (beaux-arts), the grandiose Ansonia on Manhattan's picturesque Upper West Side was one of New York's most magnificent hotels. In reality the Ansonia is more appropriately referred to as an apartment hotel, since most of its residents have been tenants rather than weekend occupants.

Built between 1899 and 1904, the Ansonia, with its

Stokes's guests also had telephones, a choice of gas or electric cooking ranges, air-conditioning and heating, ice water (in addition to hot and cold water), and three restaurants from which to choose their cuisine.

At six hundred dollars a year for a one-room apartment with bath, the Ansonia was more than a bargain: It was elegance on the cheap.

City College of New York

City College of New York City.

Founded in 1849 following an enactment of the state legislature authorizing the city and county of New York to establish a Free Academy for the city's pupils, City College was state funded in the amount of fifty thousand dollars for the necessary buildings. An additional twenty thousand annually was allocated for maintenance.

The maintenance sum seemed adequate in the beginning, especially for the Academy's first class, which consisted of 6 faculty members ministering to the educational needs of 143 students. By 1866 the reality was somewhat different, however, and the institution was rechartered as a body corporate under the name City College of New York.

Situated in the beginning on the southeast corner of Twenty-third Street and Lexington Avenue, it was later moved to Amsterdam Avenue from 136th to 140th streets in Manhattan's Washington Heights area. The main buildings pictured here were built at a cost of $4 million between 1903 and 1907. Their architectural style has been called both English Gothic (of the late Gothic period) and Collegiate Gothic. They were constructed of Manhattan schist quarried from a nearby subway excavation.

Over six hundred gargoyles decorate the buildings—mute, gnarled guardians of the intellect that resides within.

CHAPTER 4

The Times Building

Copyright 1905 by the Rotograph Co.

273   The Times Building, N. Y. City.

System (IRT), who championed the idea, guessing (correctly) that the building and the area were more important than the subway station built in its basement.

Ochs knew a good thing even before he saw it. He was sure the building would dominate the adjacent landscape, an area already fashionably occupied by the Metropolitan Opera, which opened on Fortieth and Broadway in 1883. Following closely on the Met's heels were first-run theaters and an ever-increasing assembly of music halls and cheaper entertainment houses. The addition of the Times Building in 1904 increased the influx and contributed to the Square's popularity. Proof of this was furnished by the fact that the new Times Square subway carried almost 5 million paying customers in 1905, its first year of operation.

Ochs's initial yearly lease price for the site was $27,500. It was money well spent; even the cost of demolishing the steel-framed Pabst Hotel, which occupied the area, and the $1 million cost overrun for constructing the Times Building itself did not dampen Ochs's enthusiasm for the project. In this regard his own words were prophetic: "Even though the 2.5 million that went into it caused some anxieties," he said, "it is there and it will be a monument to one man's daring."

Previously named Longacre Square, the site of the Times Building was renamed to honor both the newspaper and also its influential president and publisher, Adolph S. Ochs. Interestingly, it was August Belmont II, president of the Interborough Rapid Transit

At least for several decades Ochs was right: right on the money, right on the location.

The Great White Way

THE GREAT WHITE WAY. NEW YORK CITY

Another of New York's famous sights, whether shown on video, in newspaper or magazine format, or as seen here on the lowly postcard, is the now notorious Times Square. Historically speaking, the Square is formed by the intersection of Seventh Avenue and Broadway at Forty-second Street.

That section of Broadway which runs from Thirty-third Street to the Square was known for decades as The Great White Way. Brilliant and garish by turns, the appellation was first conferred in 1906. And now: the lights everywhere abound, everywhere beckon.

Times Square at Night

14836

This night scene of Times Square dates to circa 1940, about the date of its greatest tourist popularity. The intense lighting reveals the diversity of advertising, a longtime constant on the Square. To the viewing eye Vaudeville competes with Planters Peanuts and Coca-Cola, which vie in turn with Camels and Charlie Chaplin's name on yet another marquee. All the while Four Roses and Chevrolet oversee the cacophony of sight and sound. American in name, universal in approach and come-on.

99

Times Square

Times Square, New York City, N. Y

310 K 2477

This midcentury view of a daylight Times Square seemingly tame is less than bland (note the nude mannequins). Bond's Clothing dominates the scene both by virtue of the giant mannequins and also the overhead sign: "Every Hour 3,000 People Buy at Bond." The store offered both "Two-Trouser Suits" and "Apparel for Women"; who in their right mind could refuse the temptation to browse?

As this scenic of human activity demonstrates, Times Square was always a popular location for tourist and citizen alike. Male and female, young and old, black and white: All came to look, to spend, and to look again.

And now: Gone is Bond, gone the Hotel Astor, gone the original appearance of the Times Building itself, shaped now like a nondescript box, its one-time compelling Gothic frame hidden from aesthetic-seeking eyes.

Still happily in evidence is the majestic Paramount Building (though the Paramount Theater has disappeared from the main floor). Also available for a public look-see is the ornate 142 West Forty-second Street Building (built in 1902, replacing the original Knickerbocker Hotel), its classicism a welcome respite from much of the rest of the neighborhood. The delightful Lyceum Theater is still resplendently standing on a side street (149 West Forty-fifth Street, between Broadway and the Avenue of the Americas), its extravagant neoclassicism invigorating to the viewer, a rose within shouting distance of Times Square thorns.

But a renovation has transformed the landscape somewhat—a renovation led by the most unlikely of sources: Disney, Inc. The company has thereby added another jewel to its motion picture and theme park empire by sanitizing for purposes of profit and family entertainment the once glitzy pretension of New York's once most notorious attraction.

Macy's

Among the multiple images that come to mind when someone mentions New York City is that of the Macy's Thanksgiving Day Parade. Although it would be overstating the case to say that New York without Macy's is like a day without sunshine, it is nonetheless true that the two remain inseparable in the minds of millions of Americans.

Retired Nantucket whaling captain R. H. Macy could not have been privy to this future reality when he opened his dry-goods store at Sixth Avenue and Four- teenth Street in 1858. For the most part the Macy's building itself is rather unimpressive—solid, to be sure, but unimpressive. It is what the building contains, and its reputation, that are nonpareil. The world's largest department store, it houses ten acres of goods perishable and unperishable; items domestic, items foreign; items flippant and serious; costly and inex- pensive; mundane and exotic.

"Dry goods," indeed. "Any goods" is more like it.

Borough Hall, Brooklyn

Borough Hall, Brooklyn, N. Y.

Its history begun in the 1650s, Brooklyn was not incorporated as a city until 1834. At that point the borough wasted little time expanding and flexing its corporate muscle. Williamsburgh and Bushwick were annexed in 1855, followed by New Lots (1866); Flatbush, Gravesend, and New Utrecht (1894); and Flatlands (1896). In 1898 Brooklyn itself combined with Manhattan, Queens, the Bronx, and Staten Island, to create the New York City we recognize today.

What this unification did not do was destroy local pride; Booklynites, for example, are proud both of their borough and of their particular section of that borough, viewing themselves as separate, special people. Whether from Crown Heights or Brooklyn Heights, Fort Greene or Cobblehill, Bensonhurst or elsewhere, Brooklyn natives describe their own enclaves in superlative terms.

After a tour of the place from Prospect Park to what remains of Old Coney, from the Montauk Club to the Brooklyn Museum, and from the richness of Brooklyn Heights to the Greek Revival palace shown here, one is constrained to believe that Brooklynites might have a point. Or two.

City Hall, Brooklyn

The City Hall designation on this postcard is a misnomer insofar as the card is post-1900, but Brooklyn itself was united with Manhattan in 1898; thus it was, from that date, a borough rather than a city.

A Greek Revival structure built between 1846 and 1851, Borough Hall *was* first called City Hall. The orig-

inal plan was to build a somewhat smaller copy of Manhattan's City Hall (1802–11).

The Hall's designer was Gamaliel King, who was first a grocer, then a carpenter, before gaining recognition as an architect. The grocery store business's loss was obviously architecture's gain.

Borough Hall, Brooklyn

143   BOROUGH HALL, BROOKLYN, N. Y.

7A-H1761

This circa-1940s view of Brooklyn's Borough Hall illustrates how it stands in marked contrast to the structures in the background. The first thing to catch the eye from ground level is the six lengthy, fluted Ionic columns guarding the building's entrance. From a distance it is the cupola that attracts—even demands—attention and respect. The original cupola, constructed of wood, was destroyed by fire in 1895. This one, designed in beaux-arts style in 1898, is made of cast iron.

The allegorical figure of Justice crowning the cupola was part of the building's original design, but the statue was not executed and installed until 1897.

Westchester County Tuckahoe marble encases the structure and constitutes the broad flight of steps leading to the classic portico. The architectural style lends an air of solid and unpretentious dignity to the entire area.

Automat

From New York to Los Angeles, automated vending "restaurants" dotted the early- to mid-twentieth century landscape. Premade pies, sandwiches, casseroles, and other culinary delights resided comfortably behind glass doors, each and all awaiting selection.

Originating in Philadelphia and reaching their full growth potential in New York, Horn and Hardart's Automats were the inevitable result of an Industrial Food Service Revolution in first full blush and bloom.

People in a hurry, people on the move, people accustomed to the formality of urban living were thought to need the type of efficient, time-saving, and peopleless service that Automats provided. The only sounds were those of coins being inserted, coins making their downward spiral, arriving at their final southward destination, then a clicking as the door unlocked, ready-

ing itself for opening so that one might retrieve the savory(?) treasure.

In the more elaborate Automats, tables and chairs replicated a restaurant setting, sans the ambience and human touch.

They were ushered in prior to World War I and all but disappeared by the end of the Vietnam War era, victims both to changing public tastes and the growth of fast-food restaurant chains whose service was almost as impersonal as Automat's had been. The Fifty-seventh Street Automat seen here is gone, though the building, now renovated, serves another purpose: It became the Marboro Bookstore.

New York's remaining Automat, reported to be the world's last one as well, resides at 200 East Forty-second Street, gleefully gobbling tokens instead of coins.

Columbus Circle

Columbus Circle, Columbus and Maine Monuments, New York City.

Unlike Los Angeles, which is in almost every way a city on wheels, New York lends itself, frequently and restlessly, to pedestrian traffic. At least in part. Yes, there is an intricate, elongated, and incredible active—and actively utilized—subway system in the Big Apple. And it does have buses and cabs, plus tens of thousands of passenger cars clogging its arteries, most rudely demanding right-of-way. But an everyday/anyday analysis would lead even the most casual observer to note that New York City transacts its business on foot—or, more precisely, on millions of feet, all of them shuffling, scurrying, seemingly in motion even when standing still.

This is the impression that New York has always provided to the out-of-towner. Until, that is, he or she comes to Columbus Circle, at which time one's movements are stymied. The oft-given admonition about taking one's life into one's own hands by attempting to cross at busy intersections may first have been given to someone trying to navigate across any of a dozen venues feeding into and out of Columbus Circle. Or maybe it just seems like a dozen.

This early postcard portrait of the area belies the incredible hustle-bustle that is modern Columbus Circle reality. The bright spots to this piece of monumental congestion are monuments of another kind. They are the sculptures relating to Christopher Columbus and the Spanish-American War, which are shown here. The 1892 statue of Columbus, created by Gaetano Russo, symbolizes in dramatic and picturesque fashion the founding of this country (or, more precisely, of this continental area). Standing seventy feet high, the granite column has three bronze prows extending from it. They represent Columbus's ships, the *Nina,* the *Pinta,* and the *Santa Maria.* An image of the explorer himself commands the top of the sculpture, surveying in dignified and slightly condescending fashion what his discovery is still in the process of becoming.

The Maine monument, commemorating the sinking of that great American battleship in Havana Harbor in 1898, is more grandiose yet. A cherubic-looking figure with outstretched arms—an allegorical representation of Cuba—stands at the boat's prow. At the rear is a female representation of Peace; other figures are sculpted between these two, the more significant being a mother with a stricken child, undoubtedly a tribute to the 260 who lost their lives when the Maine exploded. Sculpted in 1913, they are the work of Attilio Piccirilli.

There is a new architectural addition to the Columbus Circle, which looms over both it and Central Park. Donald Trump, who is alternately viewed as entrepreneur and scoundrel, is at it again. The Trump International Tower, all fifty-plus gold-tinted stories of it, now occupies what was formally the Gulf and Western Building. Whether it is, as self-proclaimed, "the most important new address in the world" is open to debate.

Staging on Fifth Avenue

8987. STAGING ON FIFTH AVENUE, NEW YORK.   COPYRIGHT, 1905, BY DETROIT PUBLISHING CO.

Any protracted discussion of Fifth Avenue must at some point include certain names that have achieved icon status over the years. Astor, Vanderbilt, and Gould are among the more prominent of these, but there are others.

From midnineteenth century through the opening decades of the twentieth century, that section of Fifth Avenue that fronted Central Park was known as Millionaire's Row, in reference to the big-money cast of characters who owned slices of real estate in the area. Indeed, there were ten Vanderbilt mansions on Fifth between Fifty-seventh to Eighty-sixth streets, testament to the territory's popularity among the social and economic elite.

That architectural unity in construction and appearance was absent seemed not to bother the rich, whose primary aim was to satisfy their individual tastes, whether garish or splendid. Of more importance to them was to spend, then spend again, on furnishings and baubles, items meant to impress their wealthy friends and to awe the public.

Ballrooms in some mansions could accommodate a thousand souls, while their gargantuan kitchens were sufficiently stocked to enable them to prepare and provide gastronomical amenities for that number. Mrs. Astor, that grand dame of elitist protocol, thought it quite proper to enliven her salon with a rug woven of peacock tails. Others followed suit, making their section of New York more European and Mediterranean than American. Their extravagance was deemed eccentricism, their affectations the stuff of lovable legend.

They are gone now, probably forever if not for good. More's the pity.

Neither Fifth Avenue, nor anywhere else on earth, was to know their like again as the twentieth century propelled itself forward to the Great Depression and beyond.

Fifth Avenue On Sunday Morning

FIFTH AVENUE ON SUNDAY MORNING, NEW YORK CITY

As this postcard view informs us, Sunday morning on Fifth Avenue at the turn of the century was more than an occasion to demonstrate one's piety. For the wealthy it provided yet another opportunity to hobnob with their socially superior neighbors and to sport their finery.

True to the spirit of the Puritan Ethic, wealth and religion were viewed as two sides of the same coin. The tenets of Social Darwinism, which included the belief that capitalistically accumulated wealth was proof of one's favor with God, represented a faith all its own, one rabidly embraced by the rich.

Nowhere was this theory given more credence, or worshiped with more fervor, than on Manhattan's Fifth Avenue in that tinsel world of the long ago.

Traffic Tower, Fifth Avenue

20752

New York City.

Two streets that assist in defining Manhattan to the rest of the world are Broadway and Fifth Avenue. It is interesting to observe that each has had song lyrics devoted to it, lyrics that lead to the impression that these thoroughfares have an air of much-deserved haughtiness about them.

The perception is not altogether inaccurate. Broadway is sometimes upscale, sometimes egalitarian, and genuinely historical, all three. Fifth Avenue is a song, a candy bar, and a visual experience, all three. It is also, to give it its due, historical in the bargain—and, as regards Washington Park and a sliver of Harlem, a bit egalitarian as well.

On the other hand, millionaire trendsetters, robber barons, and other privileged elites are people, too: There are just fewer of them. Nor should their contributions be denied or denigrated. Astor and Delmonico's, Vanderbilt and Tiffany's: These are as much a part of the aura of New York as the Empire State Building, the Brooklyn Bridge, and Fiorello LaGuardia. In fact, it has taken all of these people, all of these sites, and more besides, to give New York its particular luster, its famous—and sometimes infamous—patina.

The Waldorf, after all, is more than a hotel. It is also a state of mind.

So was, and is, Fifth Avenue.

5th Avenue at Forty-second Street

71022 FIFTH AVENUE AT 42ND ST , NEW YORK

Beginning at Washington Square Park in Greenwich Village and running north, Fifth Avenue is sometimes called the "Spine" of New York. This southern connection shows that the avenue contains an iconoclastic element before its ascent toward Central Park, where it assumes a posture of exclusivity. Ending in Harlem, the street might be said, in a limited way, to have come full circle.

What does—and has—lain between these markers is a slice of New York with names familiar all over the world: The Empire State Building, St. Patrick's Cathedral, Rockefeller Center, Central Park, the Metropolitan Museum of Art (one entrance faces Fifth), Frank Lloyd Wright's Guggenheim Museum, Sak's Fifth Avenue, the Waldorf-Astoria.

And others: the New York Public Library, the University Club, the Frick Collection, the wedge-shaped Flatiron Building (the first skyscraper ever built), the Italian Renaissance-style Metropolitan Club, mansions belonging to New York's most prestigious families, shops and stores whose names have magic and the tinkle of cash registers associated with them.

One hears that Fifth Avenue is not what it was. True or not, one wonders if any other street in all the world can match its dollar value or its enchantment.

Upper Lake, Central Park

Central Park is not the first and last word about New York City. Indeed, the city's history, at least as regards Dutch habitation, predates the park's existence by more than two centuries. Nor is it the be-all and end-all of Manhattan Island itself—any more than are the Empire State Building, the New York Stock Exchange, Rockefeller Center, or any of a dozen other landmarks of world renown residing within the borough.

But what Central Park is—what it proudly and properly is—is a monument to civic planning and horticultural design. That, and a little slice of heaven in the middle of an asphalt jungle.

This is exactly how it was envisioned, even before asphalt and concrete were construction realities, by the likes of poet and newspaperman William Cullen Bryant and landscape architect Andrew Jackson Downing. After these two notables' interest was generated, all that was needed was to attract the attention of greedy Tammany Hall. And in that, as one might have expected, lay the seeds for the profiteering that followed. In 1856 Tammany's city commissioners awarded their cronies $5 million for what had previously been very inexpensive lots on which to build the park.

112

Entrance to Central Park

Copyright 1905 by the Rotograph Co.
G 7a. Entrance to Central Park, N. Y. City.

New York's population, which had seen steady, if not spectacular, increases during the 1700s, realized a monumental jump during the early and middle decades of the nineteenth century. Before the year 1850 put in its appearance, 450,000 souls inhabited the city, a threefold increase in thirty years.

The term "crowded" would seem inappropriate by today's standards, but crowded it was. Poor city planning for this type of rapid population growth spelled trouble in the form of unsanitary living conditions. This, coupled with incidences of strife within growing ethnic enclaves, created another problem: intolerance of racial and ethnic diversity.

These were reasons enough for the building of a park accessible to all. Recreation of a wholesome nature for the young, and relaxation away from the workplace and sometimes squalid and cramped neighborhoods, lent a sense of urgency to the park's creation.

The main task, after purchasing the necessary land, was the selection of architects for the project. To the city's credit they awarded the job to Frederick Law Olmsted (already employed by the city as a construction superintendent) and a youth named Calbert Vaux, whose schematic took first place in the competition.

"Greensward" was born.

The Mall, Central Park

2021—The Mall-Central Park, New York.

will be at home some time this week all well M

Souvenir Post Card Co New York and Berlin

Few areas of Central Park are as orderly or structured as The Mall. Though the means of transportation and the styles of dress shown here are radically different from what one encounters these days, two elements remain the same: the row alignment of trees and the statues of famous writers. These include the likes of Shakespeare and Sir Walter Scott; thus it is not surprising that The Mall's broad, formal walkway is called The Literary Walk.

The trees are American elms, this congregation of them being the largest in the Northeast.

Skating, Central Park

Skating Central Park, New-York.

F. B. McLean
Oct 4, 1905

It is clear from looking at this postcard that Olmsted and Vaux's desire that Central Park be a refuge free of class, race, and gender discrimination met with success, both in the early years and later. Here men, women, and children, no doubt of various ethnic backgrounds, are enjoying a winter skating excursion in a near communal atmosphere.

What the park's architects would not have appreci-ated—indeed, what they fought hard to prevent—was the incursion of office buildings, hotels, and large apart-ment structures such as the ones shown on this card.

Unfortunately, it was Tammany's lust for dollars that prevailed, as choice sites abutting the park were sold to that sometimes boon, sometimes bane of urban city planners: the modern real estate developer.

Menagerie, Central Park

Menagerie, Central Park, New York

A sad fact for Frederick Olmsted—though clearly less so for Calbert Vaux—was the erection of so many structures within Central Park. To have fought a futile battle to prevent the encroachment of buildings that could be viewed within the park was lamentable; not to have won the more significant war—to keep structures out of the park proper—was infinitely worse.

For park visitors the aesthetic impact of these "additions" is a mixed bag. Belvedere Castle (vastly deteriorated), the Gothic Revival Dairy, the cast-iron Ladies' Pavilion, and the Sheepfold are not unpleasant structures. Interestingly enough, Vaux himself designed the first two and collaborated on the Ladies' Pavilion.

The Sheepfold gave way to the magnificent Tavern on the Green, a must-see of glass-enclosed, chandeliered opulence. Not quite so sightly is the surrounding asphalt. Nor the park's parking lots; nor its overabundance of bridges and playgrounds. The complaint often heard is that what started out as a pastoral escape has become too civilized, too manicured, too well ordered.

Sleighing, Central Park

For all the complaints about what a modern Central Park may have become, there is no denying that it is a monument to civic planning and a much-needed getaway from Manhattan madness. It also continues to be a huge drawing card for the city's millions of tourists.

Its description as "the grand-daddy of all American landscaped parks" by the American Institute of Architects' Guide to New York City is both accurate and understated. Consider the wealth of locations, which include an arsenal, a castle, a sculptured fountain, numerous bridges, croquet grounds, a theater, a cottage, two ponds, a lake, a skating rink, a boathouse, pavilions, and more—including the not-insignificant Metropolitan Museum of Art.

Whatever one's recreational delights might be, there is a good chance that they may be accommodated at Central Park.

Somehow one images that Olmsted and Vaux would be pleased by these facts.

Brooklyn Navy Yard Entrance

2104— BROOKLYN Navy Yard Entrance.

Purchased by the U.S. Navy in 1801 from farmer John Jackson, the land that was to become Brooklyn's Navy Yard has had a proud history. An important servicing facility by the time of the War of 1812, its reputation—and use—continued to expand from that date. Five thousand yard workers transformed four hundred merchant marine vessels into cruisers during the Civil War. Less than a century later over seventy thousand government employees were building destroyers and battleships for use in the Second World War.

The size of the Brooklyn Navy Yard was not so very large (197 acres, of which 79 were in the water), but that space was fairly well utilized. Within its five miles of paved streets were four dry docks (measuring 326 to 700 feet), six large pontoons and cylindrical floats for salvage duty, two immense steel shipways, and a plethora of other structures: machine shops, foundries, a power plant, warehouses, a radio station, a railroad spur. Besides these were barracks for marines; two-story painted brick buildings for office quarters; a sixteen-room, two-story French Empire surgeon's house, which included a servant's wing; and a three-story former commandant's house, a federal-style building attributed to Charles Bullfinch and John Mc-Comb, Jr., which was made aesthetically appealing by an attic crowned by dormers and a widow's walk, a leaded fanlight, and an ornate cornice at the roof level.

Throw in the addition of the Greek Revival–style U.S. Naval Hospital (built in 1830–38) with its E shape, its eight classical stone piers that reach almost to the building's top, and its 125 beds, and one has a picture of the grounds before World War II. At that time both production and manpower were increased.

Carefully maintained walkways, gardens, and tennis courts complete the scenic view.

Historically speaking, the Brooklyn Navy Yard has much to commend it in addition to what has already been mentioned. The famous steamboat *Fulton* was constructed here from the inventor's design in 1814–15; the equally famous—and ill-fated—ship *Maine* was sent to sea from this yard in 1890 (guns and other trophies captured during the Spanish-American War once casually graced the grounds); and one of the first submarines (initially *Halstead's Folly,* the name was later changed to *The Intelligent Whale*) was built here in 1864 for the midnineteenth-century astronomical sum of sixty thousand dollars. Many relics of the Revolutionary War also found their way to the Brooklyn Navy Yard.

Clearly, the Navy has been more than satisfied with its forty-thousand-dollar Brooklyn investment.

The Old Ferry, Brooklyn Navy Yard

A 177   The Old Ferry, Brooklyn Navy Yard, N. Y.

For those with a sense of history, this early postcard view of the Old Ferry at the Brooklyn Navy Yard is a certain reminder of a tragedy that occurred near here.

Wallabout (Waal-Boght) Bay, reported to be the birthplace of the first Dutch child born on Long Island, was also the setting for the deaths of between seven thousand to twelve thousand American soldiers, sailors, and citizens at the hands of the British during the Revolutionary War. Their demise came about as a result of starvation, disease, general neglect, and floggings onboard prison ships, treatment received from the English sailors who occupied New York and controlled its harbor during the period.

The bones of these unfortunates were unearthed when the U.S. Navy, which purchased a section of John Jackson's farmland for a naval installation, began leveling the land to prepare for construction. A properly repulsed, indignant public, supported by the Tammany Society, demanded not only proper burial for these American patriots, but also a monument constructed to their bravery and sacrifice. Farmer Jackson himself, on some of the land where human remains had been uncovered, donated acreage near Wallabout for the purpose.

Although a proper and dignified burial ceremony (which included the presence of Honor Guards and civilian dignitaries) did take place, a monument was not forthcoming. One was finally erected at Greene Park in 1908. An appropriation of fifty-thousand dollars from the state legislature made possible this Prison Ship Martyrs' Monument, which was dedicated by President-elect William Howard Taft on November 14, 1908. The 148-foot Doric column was sculpted by Adolph Weinman under the aegis of the architectural firm of McKim, Mead, and White.

The monument yet stands; its not-so-eternal, eternal flame has been extinguished.

Revolutionary Relics at Navy Yard

Dear Rosa With much love and regards to you and your mother from E Florentine

199   REVOLUTIONARY RELICS, AT NAVY YARD, BROOKLYN. N, Y,   ILL. POST CARD CO., N. Y.

From New York City's Brooklyn Navy Yard to Muskogee, Oklahoma's Honor Heights Park, the open display of machinery and armaments relating to war was—and is—a national phenomenon. Whether the visibility of these relics represents a love of battle, or is instead a proud remembrance of personal and national sacrifice, may never be fully gauged.

What is easy to ascertain is the ubiquitous nature of the picture postcard that gives us these views, revealing yet another part of our mutifaceted selves and our wondrous universe.

General Grant

ULYSSES S. GRANT BORN IN OHIO, 1822. WENT TO WEST POINT, 1839. FOUGHT IN MEXICAN WAR, 1846. MADE COMMANDER-IN-CHIEF OF U. S. ARMY, 1864. PRESIDENT TWO TERMS, 1869-1877. DIED IN 1885.

GEN. GRANT'S TOMB. RIVERSIDE DRIVE, N. Y.

GENERAL GRANT'S CABIN
NOW IN FAIRMOUNT PARK, PHILADELPHIA. ORIGINALLY AT CITY POINT, VA., WHERE HE USED IT AS HEADQUARTERS DURING THE REBELLION.

Regarding the aesthetics of Grant's Tomb (now the General Grant National Memorial Monument), the jury of architects and landscape artists has rendered a less-than-enthusiastic judgment. Though the term "eyesore" is seldom used, neither does unstinting, effusive praise seem to be forthcoming.

This is regrettable, especially given the general's former stature as a military commander (his funeral in 1885 witnessed over seven miles of mourners stretching down Broadway). Nor is the edifice itself lacking in architectural credibility. Modeled after *Les Invalides* in Paris (which was itself made to resemble the Mausoleus's Tomb at Halicarnasus), the 150-foot-high white granite mausoleum has prestigious antecedents. It was completed in 1897.

From atop a hill, the monument's site furnishes an excellent view of the Hudson River. Its Doric columns stand guard to the entrance, while inside the Gothic structure, through the massive bronze doors and under the white dome, can be viewed (from above) the circular chamber wherein the polished twin marble sarcophagi containing the bodies of Ulysses S. and Julia Dent Grant lie at peace. Bronzes of Grant's contemporaries decorate the surroundings and offer company to the couple.

Unfortunately, lack of funding prevented the execution of all but one of the proposed exterior sculptures. This lone monument, entitled *Victory and Peace,* resides midway up the structure, directly over the Doric columns.

The modern benches (built in the 1970s) surrounding the Tomb's plaza are a good place to sit and reflect. Pity that they are so ill matched to the stateliness of the Tomb or the location.

Historic Clermont

HISTORIC CLERMONT, RIVERSIDE DRIVE, NEW YORK CITY.

Running from Seventy-second Street to 129th Street along the Hudson River on Manhattan's West Side, Riverside Drive and Riverside Park should be placed on the list of things-to-see for anyone coming to New York for the first time. Or the tenth.

Whether walking or driving, visitors will find much of the scenery marvelous, a welcome and serene respite from the rush and push of Manhattan's business and shopping districts.

First proposed in 1867 and begun in 1877, Riverside Drive and Park are still a work in progress. Initially laid out by Olmsted and Vaux (with assistance both then and later by other architects and developers), Riverside's 293 acres were dramatically altered in the 1930s by the Robert Moses administration. Moses's restructuring additions included eight new park playgrounds and 140,000 feet of walking pathways for an increase of approximately 130 acres. One hundred thirty very welcome acres.

Known as Riverside Avenue until 1908, the Drive currently features both multistoried residences and large apartment dwellings. Even some of the latter, it should be admitted, have architectural and aesthetic merit. Others, it must be admitted as well, tend toward bland-ness. Though many of the homes here are less than palatial, others are decidedly upscale (check out the Yeshiva Chofetz Chaim on Eighty-ninth). The beaux-arts town houses between 105th and 106th streets, built at the turn of the century, are certainly eye-catching as well.

Also remarkable is the Promenade, a walkway with stone parapet overlooking the river; the Seventy-ninth Street Boat Basin, which allows an invigorating walk along the river's edge; and the tree-lined serpentine drive on the upper end, which features a green island street median.

Structures along the drive that should not be missed are Grant's Tomb, Rockefeller's Riverside Church, and the prestigious Soldiers and Sailors Monument (1902), which pays homage to the New York regiments involved in the Civil War. A hundred feet in height, it rests on a granite platform with balustraded terraces beneath. Thirty-six feet are devoted to twelve Corinthian columns that form a colonnade, above which is an entablature with a frieze proclaiming "To the Memory of the Brave Soldiers and Sailors who Saved the Union," all serving to make the memorial an outstanding sight. Constructed of white marble, it does credit to its classical model, the Choragic Monument of Lysicrates in Athens.

Rockefeller Church. . .

ROCKEFELLER CHURCH. GRANT'S TOMB.
RIVERSIDE DRIVE AND GEORGE WASHINGTON
BRIDGE, NEW YORK CITY   29

Here seen dramatically in the foreground, Rockefeller Church, named for John D. Rockefeller, who paid for its construction and presented it as a gift to the city, is now called Riverside Church after its location (West 120th to 122nd on Riverside Drive).

The church has more to commend it than its location and name connection to one of New York's most prominent multimillionaires. Built in 1930 in what was even then the outdated neo-Gothic style, Riverside Church's 392-foot-high office tower (visitors can ride an elevator twenty-two stories to the top) houses the world's largest carillon (seventy-four bells). Also of spe-cial mention are the many stone carvings at the main entrance; the original sixteenth-century Flemish windows in the narthex, with scenes from the works of Albecht Dürer; and the ornamentation on the tower itself.

The addition of the south wing in 1960 was said to offer the building a more pleasing architectural appearance.

These days the church has gained a reputation for its "voice": Though Riverside Church is nominally Baptist an affiliation, its orientation is as much social and political as it is religious.

The Cathedral of St. John the Divine

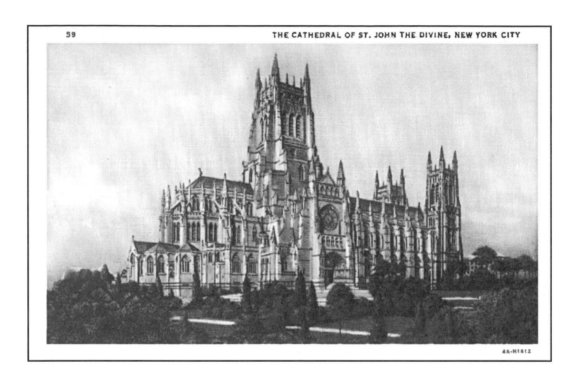

Yet another badge of distinction for New York is to be found in the dozens of historical and architecturally significant churches within the five boroughs. No other city in America comes close to challenging New York's dominance in this area.

One of those splendid edifices is the Cathedral of St. John the Divine on Amsterdam Avenue and West 112th Street. As seen on this postcard, St. John's is a strong presence against the skyline.

The building's first architects, in 1892, were Heins and Lafarge, who envisioned a Byzantine-Romanesque cathedral. By 1911 both men had died; the commission was then given to Cram and Ferguson, a move that signaled St. John's Gothic takeover. Ralph Adams Cram was the nation's most ardent supporter of Gothic Revival architecture. His belief that the French Gothic style was the only one suited for a church of St. John's size and magnitude was unflinching. It is clear from this postcard view that Cram's thoughts held sway for much of the building's architecture.

There are exceptions to this rule, however. Notable among them are the apse, choir, and crossing, which display the original Byzantine-Romanesque planning design.

Cathedral of St. John the Divine

Cathedral of St. John The Divine, New York City

This view of Morningside Heights's crown jewel appears somewhat less pretentious than the previous card portrait. Don't be misled. St. John's is impressive by almost any standards, magnificent both inside and out. The original $850,000 investment to purchase the eleven acres of land on which it sets proved to be quite a bargain.

More important, perhaps, the architecture and decoration of the church represent the pinnacle of church building in the New World. Not surprisingly, it is a cathedral second to none in size.

A note on the carved figures and other decoration: Both the statues of the martyrs on the north portal and the scenes carved beneath them are outstanding in regard both to the artistry in general and to the naturalistic style in particular. The delightful doghouse dormers that illuminate the rectory and the rectory's windows reveal an embellishment in line with medieval thought. (That is, the belief that even art should be used to honor God. In this context art was to be masterful and occasionally colorful, but always serious and respectful.)

St. John's additions and replacements are being wrought in part by a British master stonemason and his trainees.

Like New York City itself, St. John's will be truly unique, if ever finished.

Grace Church Rectory

Grace Church Rectory, N. Y. City.

Both Grace Church (88 Broadway) and the Church Rectory (804 Broadway) were the designs of architect James Renwick, Jr., who received the commission in 1843. Three years later these structures were completed.

Considered by many to be the best Gothic Revival church in New York, Grace clearly served as an architectural model for other churches not only in New York, but all across America.

Renwick, who had studied the writings of the Pugins (the great English Revival theorists), also added touches of his own that personalized the structure.

Some, however, thought the intricately contoured white marble edifice with its delicately detailed sculptures too ostentatious.

Grace Church quickly became *the* place to attend services, or perhaps more accurately, *the* place with which to be identified. Pews were sold for figures approaching fifteen hundred dollars as Grace became a center of ecclesiastical significance, a meeting place for the rich and pious.

The Gothic Revival houses, built years later, that punctuate the area create a historic and pleasing nineteenth-century mosaic.

Entrance to Greenwood Cemetery

ENTRANCE TO GREENWOOD CEMETERY, BROOKLYN, N. Y.

2005 ILLUSTRATED POST CARD CO., N. Y. Best wishes Armin.

Few of America's cemeteries are as inspiring as Brooklyn's Greenwood. Given that many, if not most, of this country's gravesites are routinely impressive in appearance, this comes as no small admission.

Then again, Greenwood is no small cemetery, either in area or in architectural, sculptural, and horticultural notability. Its 478 acres (originally 178) of forests, valleys, rolling hills, ponds, winding paths, and gorgeous lawns were the brainchild of famed surveyor and engineer David Bates Douglas. Douglas's other accomplishments included work to establish the United States/Canadian border; teaching assignments at both West Point and New York University; technical work on leading railroads and canals; and labor in an advisory capacity on numerous other engineering and architectural projects, including the design of New York University's Washington Square Campus.

Greenwood was his first—and clearly his most comprehensively executed—commission as a landscape artist. Prominent architects Frederick Olmsted and Calvert Vaux received not a few of their own ideas for the construction of Central Park and Brooklyn's Prospect Park from Douglas's Greenwood. Begun in 1838 and continuing for many years thereafter, the cemetery came to represent both natural splendor and delightful architectural eclecticism.

The Twenty-fifth Street gateway shown on this card was designed by noted architect Richard Upjohn in 1861–65. The 106-foot Gothic clock and bell tower dominate the center, rising above the gateway. The spiked arches and flying buttresses serve as excellent backdrops for the bas-relief religious sculptures lying within the recesses of the arches. The chapel and administrative offices that reside on opposite sides of the gateway are connected to it, making the complex appear as a unified whole.

Original buildings, constructed of wood, that no longer exist include several Upjohn-designed shelters. This is particularly regrettable in that their architectural styles included Italian Villa, Gothic Revival, and even Swiss Chalet. Still standing are many of the burial tombs, also in multiple styles ranging from Egyptian and Romanesque, to combinations of classical, medieval, and later designs.

Douglas and Upjohn's creation became the model not only for future cemeteries but also for the emergence of the city park system we have all come to know and value. Greenwood itself was a popular place for visitors and citizens alike. They came by the tens of thousands, attracted to the serenity, architectural wonders, and landscaped beauty. They still come, in even greater numbers.

Among the luminaries reposing in Greenwood are Currier (Nataniel), Ives (James), George Catlin, De-Witt Clinton, Horace Greeley, "Boss" Tweed, Henry Ward Beecher, and Louis Comfort Tiffany. And—oh, yes—architects James Renwick and Richard Upjohn.

Defenders Arch, Prospect Park

Photo. Only, Copyright 1905 by the Rotograph Co.
Defenders Arch, Prospect Park, Brooklyn, N. Y.

Situated on Brooklyn's Grand Army Plaza at the entrance to Prospect Park, the Soldiers' and Sailors' Memorial Arch (formally Defenders Arch) is a monument to architectural design and a tribute to the sculptor's artistry.

Commissioned in 1889 and completed in 1892, the Arch owes its artistic merit to four men: John H. Duncan, the architect also responsible for Grant's Tomb, and sculptors Frederick MacMonnies, Thomas Eakins, and William O. Donovan. Others making contributions are Phillip Martiny, Stanford White, and Alexander Phimster Proctor.

Initially the Arch (French, *Arc*) was without ornamentation. It could not so remain and be a true Arc in the historic, romantic sense, which that term implies. Like Paris's Arc de Triomphe, to which it is often compared, the sculpture lacks nothing in achieving magnificence—after, that is, the sculptors had defined it.

In 1895 sculptors Eakins and Donovan created the equestrian bas-relief bronze panels of Presidents Lincoln and Grant seen inside the Arch (Martiny was responsible for the spandrel abutments). Stanford White's Classical Revival additions consist of Doric columns on the Park side, displaying bronze eagles on globes. Proctor's bronze Panthers (1898), which ornament the Third Street pedestals, are certainly also worthy of mention. The most remarkable effect, however, is that created by MacMonnies (1898), who, as fortune would have it, was Brooklyn born. What he gave the Arch was additional aesthetics, along with a presence denoting character, strength, and formidability.

The four-horse chariot (called a quadriga) dominates not only the top of the Arch but the entire Plaza skyline. It is obvious that MacMonnies operated unashamedly on classically realistic lines, in this instance to compelling effect. His *Army* and *Navy* sculptures on the left and right, respectively, offer vistas no less than engrossing. Here again, classical allusions abound, creating wonder within the viewer, almost overwhelming the senses as the imagination is forced into play. Battle begets patriotism, begets images of right becoming might, begets visions of crusades against moral darkness and tyrannical oppression.

More than compelling, the view is almost intoxicating.

Sheep in Prospect Park

SHEEP IN PROSPECT PARK, BROOKLYN, N.Y.

These sheep walking over Brooklyn's Prospect Park in the days of the Long Ago knew what millions of humans were to discover: This 526 acres of nature's contoured and manicured best are a perfect pastoral place of escape and refuge from the sometime craziness of the city that surrounds it.

Prospect Park's construction was contemplated as early as 1859, but the work was delayed by the onset of the Civil War. Finally begun in 1866, it was well worth the wait. Well-known architects Frederick Olmsted and Calvert Vaux had gained a national reputation for Manhattan's Central Park, their previous project. They had also learned a few things from a careful study of Greenwood Cemetery. All of this learning and technique were applied toward the creation of Prospect Park.

Prospect was built to accommodate both pedestrian and vehicular traffic, the former being the primary, mid-nineteenth century concern. Arched overpasses carried the carriages, while foot pounding took place below.

The Park was quite a series of sites and sights to traverse, laid out to accommodate a vast lake (fifty-seven acres), paths leading through the obligatory wooded areas, and a large meadow for relaxation in the form of kite flying, ball games, picnicking, sunbathing.

Of all the attempts at egalitarianism, the American park system may, in the end, prove to be the greatest social leveler. Popular entertainments may or may not appeal to all classes of society; even Coney Island, temptress of rich and poor alike, was avoided by some individuals who resented the middle- and lower-class atmosphere they assumed prevailed there. But a magnificent city park, which offers not only natural beauty but the cultural sophistication of appearances by operas and symphonies, is a lure even the aristocrat finds too appealing to reject.

Among the many things to see at Prospect Park are the ninety acres of Long Meadow; the Boathouse, a superb two-story terra-cotta structure of neoclassical design (1904); McKim, Mead, and White's elegant Grecian Shelter (1905), with its twenty-eight Corinthian columns; historic Litchfield Villa, built in 1856 and therefore already in the Park proper (and as good an example of an Italian Villa as one is likely to see in this or any other setting in the United States); and the Lefferts Homestead, a delightful Dutch Colonial farmhouse, built in the late 1700s and moved to the park in 1918.

Gone, sadly, are the rustic shelters, but the restoration of Vaux's Oriental Pavilion (1874) after destruction by fire is a refreshing sight. The restored Music Pagoda (1888) is, likewise, a welcome addition.

There is more, including statuary (H. K. Brown's Lincoln is noteworthy), a World War I memorial, the Soldiers' and Sailors' Memorial Arch, a landing shelter, and a boulder bridge.

An interesting elimination was Mount Prospect, the hill that gave the park its name.

Jumel Mansion

A 40 a. Jumel Mansion, erected 1758, N. Y. City.

The Morris-Jumel Mansion is a Manhattan landmark. Well it should be, for it is the oldest building on the island, as well as the only pre-Revolutionary structure there. Built in 1765 by Colonel Roger Morris, a member of New York's British Executive Council, the mansion conforms to the Georgian style of architecture.

In some ways the mansion is less than it seems: The stonework on the facade is imitation, the front corner quoins are made of wood rather than stone, and the rear facade is covered with cost-saving shingles.

Nonetheless, the structure was useful enough to have several occupants over the years. When Morris fled to England at the outbreak of the Revolutionary War (leaving his wife to manage affairs), the house was used first by George Washington as his headquarters, then for a longer period by the British general Sir Henry Clinton when the English captured the island. It was also the residence of Baron von Knyphausen and his Hessian troops.

The Morris property was confiscated after the war in 1783 and became, for a short while, a fashionable inn. It was then purchased by a successful French wine merchant named Stephen Jumel, who moved into the mansion with his not-quite-socially-acceptable wife, Eliza, who was rumored to have been romantically linked to George Washington prior to her marriage. Jumel did a partial renovation of the residence in the then-popular federal style. Upon his death Eliza remained in the house, later marrying Aaron Burr, who had, many years earlier, killed Alexander Hamilton in a duel. One doubts if Burr remembered many of the details at this point in his life: He was eighty and not in the best of health, either physically or mentally.

The mansion's later ties to history were not so grandiose, but more fitting to its age: It became a museum in 1903 after its purchase by the city in response to a request from its last private owners.

It now stands proudly under the guardianship of the Washington Headquarters Association, which maintains it with immaculate care.

Herald Square

G 35b. Herald Square, N. Y. City

This pre-1920 view of Herald Square is reminiscent of much of America in those early-twentieth-century years. Horse-drawn conveyances, street cars, bustling pedestrian traffic: This could be Boston or Philadelphia, Chicago or Detroit. Indeed, it could be London or Paris.

Turning the clock back another thirty years to the 1870s would have revealed a somewhat different, somewhat less wholesome, reality. Herald Square in that era was the center of an area where sin and vice operated on a day-and-night, cash-talks basis. Called New York's Tenderloin, the area (roughly between Fifth Avenue and Hell's Kitchen) was rife with prosti-

tution, gambling houses, dance halls, inexpensive hotels, and cafés catering to every taste.

New York's political machine, Tammany Hall, had its own hand deep into the till: The machine was the economic sponsor and patron of some of these establishments.

Within twenty years Herald Square would become a bastion of both upper- and middle-class shopping. But not before the 1880s; in fact, it was not till the end of the nineteenth century that the area was called Herald Square. Previously the Square was not a location where proper members of society would want to be seen.

Herald Square

Herald Square, Broadway and Sixth Avenue, New York City.

When George M. Cohan immortalized this piece of New York commercial real estate in song, he did so in response to the business that Herald Square generated rather than to the aesthetics of the location itself. Herald Square's reputation as a shopping district is well earned: Within the physical triangle that defines its geography were to be found such names as Gimbel's (since renovated for a new Abraham and Straus), Macy's, and Saks.

Gone are some of the hotels that added glitter to the night life (the McAlpin, the Pennsylvania) and defined the area as an interesting locale to seek entertainment of after-hours variety. The Pennsylvania's demise—or, rather, change in appearance and name—is particularly to be mourned, given that it was considered by many to be the fashion center of New York's garment industry, a place for buyers and sellers to congregate, and for fashion shows to parade the latest in haute couture.

Herald Square received its name from the *Herald* newspaper, which moved its building plant and offices—built by the ubiquitous firm of McKim, Mead, and White—into the area in 1894. When the newspaper again changed locations and was later razed in 1921, nothing remained. Even the beautifully detailed bronze landmark sculptures of Minerva the goddess, seemingly supervising the activities of two workers (affectionately nicknamed Stuff and Guff) striking a huge bell to toll the time, were taken to City University before finally being returned to a place of prominence on the Square.

Rising like a Phoenix from Herald Square's ashes is the five-square-block Jacob Javits Convention Center, sprawling and intimidating with its glaring black windows, yet strangely inviting and dominating.

Also in evidence is Macy's, arguably the most well-known department store in the world. Its Palladian facade graces the exterior, while occasional shopping madness occasioned by teeming throngs may still be witnessed inside. Recently added to Macy's offerings is an autograph and coin shop, evidence that Macy's is attempting to remain an island of enchantment and adventure, a river ever ready to be navigated.

The area also includes (besides a close-up view of the Empire State Building) a number of architecturally interesting buildings, among which are the Greenwich Savings Bank, New York's General Post Office, and the Manhattan Center (the former New Yorker Hotel).

And shops. And restaurants. And more.

Herald Square has been around the world—and come back.

City Hall Park

This quaint, almost rustic, image of City Hall Park at the turn of the century reflects a time and a mindset some distance removed from the New York City of the 1990s. The area, previously called The Commons, was precisely that: an outdoor arena where citizens often met to protest or support, often in an enthusiastic if not downright boisterous manner. Examples of this abound: The five Liberty Poles defiantly planted here in the decade between 1766 and 1776 by the Sons of Liberty to protest British sovereignty; the Flour Riot of 1837, when six thousand angered citizens rebelled against a rise in the price of flour—and subsequently bread—by breaking into flour stores; the 1857 police debacle when the ousted Municipal Police clashed in combat with the Metropolitan Police, who were authorized by the state legislature to replace them.

Other examples are more tame, as when the Declaration of Independence was read for the first time, in the presence of George Washington, to a public gathering in 1776. Or the 1900 ceremony that celebrated the beginning of construction for what was to become the most elaborate subway system on earth.

Interestingly, the area had served a number of purposes over the years, being the site of a jail, an almshouse, a barracks for British soldiers, even an ex-ecution ground. All this before the erection of the county courthouse, the Municipal Building, and the U.S. Courthouse.

City Hall itself is an architectural throwback, and as such, as delightful to view as the trees and flowers that decorate the park. So too are the statues, which add a further sense of history and dignity to the place. Nathan Hale, properly bronzed, clad in longcoat, is presented as unpretentious and unassuming, if slightly—and correctly—above reproach by his British captors. Frederick MacMonnies was the talented sculptor who offered this immortal portrayal of that rare man whose behavior matched his rhetoric. The statue was completed in 1890, unveiled in 1893.

Horace Greeley has also been suitably bronzed in City Hall Park. Seated in a chair with printed material at hand and a look of contemplation and sadness upon his countenance, Greeley is presented as the archetypical newspaper editor. This reflective soul acted out his conscience and his feelings on paper in the *New York Tribune,* which he founded in 1841 and editored for thirty years thereafter. Legend has it that Greeley admonished his juniors to "Go west, young man, go west." Thankfully, for New York readers, Greeley did not accept his own advice.

Hall of Records, City Hall Park

The bad news is that this postcard representation fails to do justice to the building it pictures. The good news is that the building is standing still, a visual delight both outside and within.

Cost overruns and crooked politics overplayed their roles in the construction of the Hall of Records, but in this instance the machinations wound up being part of the process whereby the structure came to life.

Reform mayor William Strong appointed established architect John R. Thomas to oversee the project. Thomas had previously extended and refurbished the New York Stock Exchange Building and was known as honest and efficient in all his dealings, proof being furnished by the $1 million he had reportedly saved the state by his reputable practices with suppliers and contractors.

However, when Tammany regained control of City Hall in 1898, Thomas had nothing but problems from them. These included demands for new plans and new bids from Mayor Van Wyck, and the involvement of lawless county judges who argued for the addition of a new courthouse to be placed alongside the expanding Court of Records. For Thomas the unrelenting

pressure exerted by Tammany proved too great: He died of a heart attack in 1901.

The project was then given to a pair of unscrupulous characters named Horgan and Slattery. The costs quickly rose from an original projection of $2 million to the final 1908 completion tabulation of $8 million. Moreover, Arthur J. Horgan and Vincent J. Slattery were petty as well as avaricious, the former trait exhibiting itself in their inability to release information to the proper authorities on schedule, or to maintain anything approaching cordial relations with the project's sculptors.

No matter; overall, the results are impressive. Though some of the upstairs marble is not marble, but rather "plaster enrichment"—and though costs for material and the time estimated to complete the job were both outrageously underestimated—the sculptures of Phillip Martiny, and the beaux-arts siena marble staircase designed by Thomas before his demise, are touches of the highest quality. So, too, the free-standing sculptures of local historical figures, including Peter Stuyvesant and DeWitt Clinton. The rostra on the corners of the fourth story and the abundance of scroll framing are further testaments to Thomas's skills—in this case his social skills in creating a positive attitude among his stone carvers and sculptors, who were then able to endure the harangues of Messrs. Horgan and Slattery.

The Corinthian columns, welcome additions to many turn-of-the-century edifices, are particularly appropriate here, as they point the way to all the ornamentation above them.

The building's interior is a showcase, as well, with decorative wall work, impressive skylighting, marble fireplaces, and massive wooden staircases, doors, and more, all having been chiseled, burled, or otherwise artistically accomplished. Of special merit in this latter regard is the Surrogate Court, housed within the building.

City Hall, New York City

City Hall, N. Y. City

No. 72. National Art Views Co. N. Y. City.

As any visitor to New York can attest, the five boroughs may be justifiably proud that they have retained as many of their nineteenth- and early twentieth-century structures as any other city in America. That preservation includes the elegant nineteenth-century Manhattan City Hall Building pictured here. The third town center in Manhattan history to be built, it has proved to be the best.

Designed by the architectural firm of Joseph Mangin (a Frenchman) and John McComb (a Scot) between 1803 and 1812, the exterior style is a mixture of federal and French Renaissance, while the interior has elements of American Geogian. Mangin is generally credited with being the designer of the exterior, whereas McComb is thought to be responsible for much of the inside of the structure.

The front and side facades of the two-story building were covered with white Massachusetts marble, but the rear employed the use of New Jersey brownstone, a fifteen-thousand-dollar cost-cutting measure insisted upon by the city fathers. Their thinking was to the effect that no one would ever see the north side of the building; they did not project the city's growth any farther than this point.

City Hall's interior is just short of awe inspiring. The twin spiral staircases winds to the second floor, where ten Corinthian columns support a majestic dome surrounded by Renaissance swag and rosette detailing.

Above the attic is the clock tower, built in 1831; the cupola was topped by a wooden female figure of Justice, which was redone in copper when the building was refurbished at the turn of the century. The tower and attic had been destroyed in 1858 by fire. At that time, and later, alterations were made that changed the buildings's architectural complexion; the restoration undertaken around 1900 restored the original look.

A Governor's Room was established on the second floor in 1814, to be used for important official functions. The two most significant occurrences inside the building were the laying in state of former presidents Abraham Lincoln and Ulysses S. Grant. Both were placed outside the Governor's Room. Lincoln's twenty-four-hour stay in City Hall witnessed 120,000 people paying their respects to the slain leader.

In the mid-1950s residents of Manhattan refused to let their architectural treasure fall to the wrecking ball, an action thought necessary because industrial pollution and the ravages of time and weather had left the building in a sad state of disrepair. The restoration was a lengthy and expensive process: Fifteen thousand individual pieces of Alabama limestone were secured by rods to the entire exterior, and the brownstone in the basement was replaced with Missouri red granite.

From the delicate manner in which the building stands in marked contrast to the structures surrounding it, to the attention to detail evident in everything from plaster work to moldings, New York's City Hall is clearly an architectural jewel in miniature.

CHAPTER 5

The Siegel-Cooper Department Store

The Siegel-Cooper Department Store, New York.

This Chicago-based company took New York by storm with the opening in 1896 of the store shown here. Fifteen and one-half acres of interior space make this beaux-art-style edifice huge by any department store's standards. The 150,000 shoppers who swarmed into Siegel-Cooper on opening day disembarked from an El train one floor above the street (the track is plainly visible on this early postcard).

Three thousand clerks greeted, catered to, and pointed directions for them. A fountain in the central atrium of the ground floor produced a jet of water accompanying a statue of the Republic. This statue is a smaller version of the one modeled by Daniel Chester French at the Chicago Exposition in 1893. The owner wisely commissioned French to replicate the masterpiece rather than securing the services of a lesser sculptor. The piece now resides at California's Forest Lawn Cemetery.

By the end of its first decade, the novelty of Siegel-Cooper had worn sufficiently thin, and sales had reached the point where the owners found it necessary to sell their retail behemoth. Their previous refusal to move north from the six-hundred block of Sixth Avenue to Twenty-third or Twenty-fourth street shopping districts condemned the building to white-elephant status.

During World War I Siegel-Cooper's became a military hospital. Since then preservationists have lobbied in favor of the building, which has kept it from being destroyed.

Sadly gone are the dome-shaped top and the rows of flags pictured here.

Boy's High School, Brooklyn

Boys' High School, Brooklyn, N.Y.

Erected in 1891, this Romanesque Revival building was located on Marcy Avenue in Brooklyn. Its institutional appearance, popular at the time, gives every indication that its function was a serious one. Indeed, architect Henry Richardson sought this effect.

With bells, towers, round-arched windows, and omnipresent gables, he achieved it. Austere, almost forbidding, it is also grand in its solidity, its obvious commitment to permanence and craftsmanship, and its prominent stature against the skyline.

Even Brooklyn's Board of Education must have cherished the memories it contained. Rather than demolishing it, they chose to preserve the building, and though no longer a school, it continues to serve educational purposes.

The Aquarium

The Aquarium, New York.

Perhaps in views such as this, early picture postcards more than prove their historical utility.

The Aquarium, designed in 1896 and demolished in 1942, was a slice of Americana cut from the mold of a Norman Rockwell painting. One can look at this picture and easily imagine the tourists tramping inside; the young, old, black, white, men and women; the sailors with their favorite girl of the moment; the students and teachers; the anthropologists and other men of science; the mildly curious, the otherwise bored.

The facility and its exhibits attracted as many as forty-thousand visitors a day. The Aquarium temporarily housed, entertained, and educated them all over the years.

And then the wrecking ball appeared. But not before the publishers and producers of picture postcards could immortalize and freeze-frame all the imagery that a sight of the old Aquarium stimulates.

Aquarium, Battery Park

Aquarium; Battery Park.   New York.

View from my window at Em. House.

This long-distance view of the Aquarium illustrates how well—and, considering its contents, how appropriately—the structure blended with its immediate surroundings.

Originally the area was called the Southwest Battery, its function to serve as harbor defense. After the War of 1812 its was renamed Castle Clinton. It did not, however, see enemy action, none of its twenty-eight guns ever having been fired in battle. Initially separated from Manhattan by three-hundred feet of water, it was later connected to the island by a landfill.

The federal government turned the fort over to the city in 1823, and it has since witnessed various revivals and uses, converted at first to Castle Garden, a concert hall and gathering place for fashionable people and events. Enrico Caruso, Jenny Lind—who made her American debut here in 1850—and others of repute graced and dignified the Gardens with their presence and their performances. In 1855 it became an immigrant landing depot, eventually processing over 7 million people through its portals in more than forty years of operation, and finally ending the nineteenth century by becoming an aquarium in 1896 after a remodeling job by McKim, Mead, and White.

Its success as an aquarium is demonstrated by several facts. By the end of 1937 over seventy-six million people had toured the Aquarium, examining its manifold exhibits. Enclosed within the three-story circular building were 8,877 fishes, 872 invertebrates, 198 reptiles, 65 amphibians, and 12 birds. Contained within its massive interior were seven large floor pools, eighty-eight large glass-fronted wall tanks, eighty-three smaller tanks, and twenty-nine large reserve tanks that housed specimens not on exhibition.

When the Aquarium was closed in 1942, its upper section was destroyed, but the original eight-foot-thick walls and gun embrasures remain as part of the Castle Clinton National Monument (established in 1946), which is under the jurisdiction of the National Park Service.

Memorial to Father Duffy

116A.— MEMORIAL TO FATHER DUFFY

FATHER DUFFY

TIMES SQUARE   NEW YORK

Few men—or women—have impacted a city in a more profound, positive manner than Father Francis P. Duffy did New York. Long before Edmond O'Brien starred as the "Fighting Chaplain" of New York's Sixty-ninth Regiment during World War I, Duffy had established his big-hearted and pugnacious reputation. His Holy Cross Church was refuge to many among the lower classes and witnessed its share of thieves and prostitutes along with GIs, actors, writers, and other creative types. Father Duffy looked into their hearts, not into their wallets or their past.

His Byzantine-style church still stands, as does the statue. The latter resides at the northern triangle of Times Square, appropriately named Duffy Square. It faces the back of a statue of George M. Cohan, the famous stage performer, composer, writer, and director. This too is fitting insofar as each represented a commitment both to America and to the "common" people who inhabit her shores.

Grand Central Station

Copyright 1906 by the Rotograph Co.

G 60a Grand Central Station, N. Y. City.

interior in the United States, it also set the architectural style for other stations for many years to come.

Completed in 1871 by architect John B. Snook (who had, coincidentally, built America's first great department store), the structure was both huge and elegant. Built with the single-span concept of St. Pancras, Grand Central proved to be more efficient than other train stations because of the added room that this concept permitted. The south and west facades utilized eye-appealing red brick with stone quoins, cast iron being used in the mansard roof, the crestings, and other detailing. The Second Empire roofline was reminiscent both of the Louvre and the Tuileries, a fact that must have captured Vanderbilt's nouveau riche fancy.

The semicircular metal and glass arch overlooking and spanning the train yard may not have been particularly innovative when compared with European models. It was, however, most impressive for 1870s America.

Trouble appeared after the death of Vanderbilt in 1887 and the assumption of his empire by son William H. Even more visionary and expansionist than his father, William increased the family fortune threefold. But the ballooning of train traffic with the passage of time strained Grand Central, necessitating the addition of three floors (bringing the height to six stories). Architect Bradford Gilbert also added to the station's visual luster with the application of stone-resembling rusticated stucco over the exterior facade. He added, as well, two stately copper-clad cupolas.

Unfortunately, the traffic strain was only momentarily reduced. A safety concern factor was likewise ill addressed and was in part responsible for the untimely deaths of fifteen passengers on the freezing morning of January 8, 1902, when two steam locomotives collided on the Park Avenue tunnel approach to Grand Central.

What is pictured on this postcard is not the Grand Central Station that is so revered in New York City today, but rather, the earlier Grand Central Station built in 1871 and remodeled in 1898—the station that was the brainchild of the storied Vanderbilts.

A bit of historical background is in order. Railroad magnate and capitalistic entrepreneur Commodore Cornelius Vanderbilt had in mind, as early as the 1850s, the construction of the largest railroad station in the world. In this endeavor he did not succeed; London's St. Pancras, among others, was bigger. But Vanderbilt did accomplish a few things: his hundred-foot-high, two-hundred-foot-wide, six-hundred-foot-long Grand Central Station was not only the largest train terminal

The first casualty of the wreck was a direct one: Steam engines were totally banned in Manhattan by 1908. The last victim was the original structure itself. J. Wilgus, chief engineer for all bridge and terminal construction for the railroads, introduced his master plan to solve the traffic and real-estate problems. The result: In 1913 an even more stately Grand Central Terminal (that is, the end of the line, not just another station or stop) was born, a structure of magnificence.

Empire State Building

EMPIRE STATE BUILDING, NEW YORK CITY

The Empire State's exterior, covered with limestone, granite, aluminum, and nickel, is slightly art deco but fully pleasing, its aesthetic series of setbacks making it a visual dessert for the eyes. The entire structure, all 1,250 feet of it, is solid, almost austere in appearance, yet entrancing. It is this dichotomy, this business of being both forbidding yet strangely welcoming, of being graceful yet dominating, that makes the building such a compelling vista.

The elevator goes up eighty-six floors, but there are another fourteen for the tower and mast. A mixture of gray and red marble are in abundant evidence at the entrance halls, the lobby, and the elevator concourses. A special feature on the wall at the Fifth Avenue entrance hall is a map of New York State and an aluminum representation of the building with the golden rays of the sun extending in every direction behind it.

Built on the former site of the Waldorf-Astoria Hotel, the Empire State Building had as its chief architect William F. Lamb of the firm of Shreve, Lamb, and Harmon. Known for no-nonsense efficiency and the use of clean lines, Lamb here created his most enduring and endearing masterpiece. Much of the credit for the building's practicality of design must also go to its builder, John J. Raskob, multimillionaire General Motors executive and stockholder. Planned as an office building with a secondary thought to making it the world's largest structure, Empire State was initially—and for a number of years after—unable to locate enough renters to fill the building. The Depression was in full depressing sway, more business owners filing bankruptcy than expanding their operations.

Happily, Empire State endured. Perhaps New Yorkers discovered—as King Kong had—that this was one skyscraper worth getting to know, up close and personal.

It is perhaps the case that there have been more words written about the Empire State Building than any other building on earth. It is also perhaps the case that the structure would feel at home in no other city on the planet than the one in which it resides. They were—again, perhaps—made one for the other: Gotham and Empire State, Empire State and Gotham.

One thing is taken out of the realm of "perhaps" and placed squarely into the world of that which is certain: By any conceivable earthly standards, the Empire State Building is an inspiring structure. At the time of its completion in 1931, it was the tallest building in the world; and though its height has been exceeded, no other building will ever dwarf it, either in reputation or in sheer size. It is that big.

Fort Washington

FORT WASHINGTON, WASHINGTON HEIGHTS,
NEW YORK CITY

This part of Manhattan where the island narrows is crowded with apartments, museums, cultural institutions, even a university. There is Trinity Cemetery with its revered deceased, including Madame Jumel (the Jumel Mansion is also in Washington Heights); Clement Moore, author of "'Twas the Night before Christmas"; a few Vanderbilts and Astors; and a tomb for John Jacob Audubon, the famous naturalist. There is the world-famous Museum of the American Indian, the American Numismatic Museum, the National Institute of Arts and Letters, the Hispanic Society of America. There is Boricua College, formally the American Geographic Society. There is the majestic George Washington Bridge spanning the Hudson River, once the world's largest suspension bridge (before the Golden Gate was built), still called the world's most beautiful bridge. There is the Alexander Hamilton Bridge, the Audubon Research Park, the Columbian-Presbyterian Medical Center.

And Fort Washington Park, so named to commemorate the Battle of Fort Washington fought in 1776. This November 16 encounter witnessed the deaths of 54 Americans and the capture of 2,634 more, as contingents of Hessian and British troops stormed from all directions, firing also from warships on the Hudson. It was a total rout, the British occupying the Fort as they had earlier captured the city of New York, not disgorging from the area until the end of the Revolutionary War.

Hayden Planetarium

Hayden Planetarium, 81st and Central Park West, New York City   195

62285

Located at the Eighty-first Street termination of the American Museum of Natural History, the Hayden Planetarium is at once more than the architecture that houses it.

Adding validity to the belief that the natural universe is as wondrous as it is portrayed on the various *Star* *Trek* incarnations, the Planetarium offers unforgettable panoramic shows that dramatize the movements of the stars, the planets, the universe itself. It is quite an accomplishment, especially when one remembers that these images were being produced decades before the term "virtual reality" had become part of the lexicon.

Union Square

New York. Union Square. *Don't wait for me, it will be impossible for me to go to-night. Hope you will have a good time. Love Adele*

Copyright by R. F. Turnbull N.Y

Few areas of the city have undergone as many changes as has Union Square. From grand residential setting in the early to mid nineteenth century, to theatrical district beginning in the 1850s with the opening of the Academy of Music, to a center for radical activity, to a haven for drug dealers and derelicts, to a reclaimed project on the rehabilitation upswing. It has, in every way, been to heaven, been to hell, and come back.

Union Square began its civic life in 1811 as Union Place, so named because the area was a connecting link between Bloomingdale Road (now Broadway) and Bowery Road (now Fourth Avenue). It was also referred to locally as "the Forks," a rustic reference to streets feeding in and out of the location. For decades thereafter Union Place was a fashionable habitation of such social luminaries as Daniel Drew, James Roosevelt, and Robert Goelet. A heavy iron fence, like that at Gramercy Park, encircled their park, the gates being secured at sundown.

The reputation of the site was further enhanced by the addition of the aforementioned Academy of Music and, later, the famous Delmonico's Restaurant, Tiffany's Jewelry Store, and a host of other elitist establishments, including B. Altman's, Brentano's Literary Emporium, Daniel's, and, for the middle-class crowd, Siegel-Cooper.

By the turn of the century, however, the mood and flavor of the neighborhood had begun to change. The complexion was becoming less fashionable, less grandiose. Leaving were the more genteel stores; into the breech came the needle trades, because of the area's proximity to the fashionable shopping district on one side, and to the Lower East Side, with its abundant supply of cheap immigrant labor.

By this time the once wealth-ridden neighborhood was home to a wide variety of social types. Struggling artists of all descriptions shared the area (many, like Max Weber and Walter Pack, went on to carve a successful niche for themselves within the artistic community). Real estate value had shrunk, the tenement dwellers—many of whom frequented the burlesque houses and other cheap entertainment and service-oriented establishments that were sprouting up in ugly profusion—proliferating.

Not surprisingly, Union Square became a center of social protest. Agitation and rebellion against the existing social structure that kept the rich and powerful in positions of strength, while the poor and uneducated were useful only as laborers and consumers, fed the machinery of trade unionism and was fertile ground for the growth of socialistic and communistic doctrine.

The statuary at Union Square has been its one constant for the past century, lending dignity and instilling pride. The equestrian bronze of George Washington, built in 1856 by sculptor Henry Kirke Brown, graces Fourteenth Street, marking the spot where General Washington was warmly received by a throng of faithful citizens. Brown was also the sculptor of the Abraham Lincoln bronze (1868) that was given to the city by the Union League Club in 1931. The 1876 pedestal-mounted statue of the Marquis de Lafayette, who fought with George Washington, was designed and constructed by Frederic Bartholdi, creator of the Statue of Liberty.

Firemen's Exhibition

NEW YORK. FIREMEN'S EXHIBITION AT UNION SQUARE.

Union Square's former reputation as a hotbed of social unrest and protest is well deserved. The role that the police played in the drama is instructive: Their presence often made of a bad situation a worse one. Three prominent examples present themselves.

On the night in 1927 when the two anarchists, Sacco and Vanzetti, were executed, a small procession that formed on the Square was forcibly broken up, resulting in injury to several marchers; in 1929 an "anti–police brutality" demonstration engineered by the Communist Party was dispersed by the city police, but not until severe injuries and physical impairment were visited upon many of the protestors and twenty-seven of their number, nine of them children, were taken into custody; in March of 1930 more than thirty-five thousand unemployed workers and their friends congregated on the Square with the intention of listening to fiery rhetoric and then marching on City Hall. Breaking up the parade led to head cracking, kicking, and clubbing, until more than one-hundred persons were injured and thirteen arrests were recorded.

Protest and rhetoric were two staples of Union Square for decades, beginning in the teens. And no wonder: By the 1930s both the Socialist and Communist parties were entrenched in the Square and published their newspapers there. Also present was the Rand School of Social Science, the International Labor Defense, the American League for Peace and Democracy, the American Civil Liberties Union, the International Workers Order—and more.

Scenes such as the Firemen's Exhibition pictured here were also part of the Square's picturesque history. So too the now famous May Day Parade.

Today the area is being transformed from the unsavory image it acquired when drug dealers and derelicts took over Union Square Park in the 1960s. A late 1980s reclamation project has attempted to alter that reputation. There is now a Green Market, where farmers and others bring their goods and produce to sell on the Square four days a week.

Columbia University

Columbia University, New York.

Copyright 1910 by Geo. P. Hall & Son. New York.

153

Beginning its academic life as King's College in 1754, Columbia University did not get a name change until after the Revolutionary War, when it became Columbia College. The "University" designation was not officially applied by the city until 1896, the state legislature approving the title in 1912.

By that time Columbia had made two residence changes. The first was from its original location between Church, Barclay, and Murray streets fronting the Hudson River, to the former home of the deaf and dumb on Madison Avenue (1857); then to its present site on West 116th Street between Broadway and Amsterdam Avenue in Manhattan (1897).

The University grew slowly in the beginning. In fact, only 107 students occupied it after ninety years of operation. By 1892 the student body had swelled to 1,600, with a teaching staff of 80 instructors. It has continued apace ever since—as would befit an institution of its standing.

The honors and superlatives abound: Columbia has the oldest and largest school of library science in America; the prestigious Columbia School of Journalism was the only graduate school of its kind in the world. Columbia's library was the third-largest university library in America, its forty thousand volumes on architecture the largest collection of books on that topic. Columbia's graduates have included U.S. presidents, Supreme Court justices, scientists, and noted experts in almost every field of human endeavor.

Columbia was the sixth college established in the colonies, its early graduates including John Jay (1764), Robert Livingston (1765), Gouverneur Morris (1768), Alexander Hamilton (1778), and DeWitt Clinton (1786).

Architecturally speaking, Columbia is diffuse in styles, owing in large part to the different designers who worked on the buildings. McKim, Mead, and White received the commission, McKim beginning the task in 1895 on the structures seen here. His plan called for interconnected courtyards, terraced in such a way as to take the topography into account. He also wanted the main buildings to be designed along classical or beaux-arts lines. What occurred instead, apart from the grandeur of Low's Library and St. Paul's Chapel (1907), were a series of structures of red brick and limestone trim of the Italian Renaissance style, and a mishmash of types whose overall banality has been the subject of disparaging remarks by students and architects alike.

Low Memorial Library

KINGS COLLEGE FOUNDED IN THE PROVINCE OF NEW YORK

THE LIBRARY OF COLUMBIA UNIVERSITY

154

Built first, but built to last, Low Memorial Library is both stately and demanding, demanding to be seen, then seen again.

Completed in 1897, the library was named for the father of Columbia president Seth Low, later New York City mayor, who was also a graduate of the institution (class of 1870). A successful businessman, Low contributed a million dollars (one-third of his personal fortune) for its construction. What he received for his investment was more than a mere building. Though the structure failed as a library and was used instead for administrative purposes (1934), its reputation as one of the most architecturally superlative of New York's many architecturally superlative buildings is praiseworthy in the extreme.

Some details: The gray Indiana-limestone-encased structure was planned as a Greek cross. The first arm included the ground entrance, the president's office, and the trustees' room. The Avery architectural and law libraries each had their own arm, with the catalog and delivery room being the fourth arm.

An impressive sky-blue dome tops a beaux-arts interior, which includes a visually magnificent octagonal hall. Here was the main reading room, with tables arranged in concentric rings; seminar rooms reside on the second floor, and lecture halls occupy the third.

Nor is the building's exterior less than inspiring. The three tiers of steps not only lead to the building but also serve as connecting links between one part of the campus and another, specifically to those buildings beside or behind Low's. They may also be a destination in themselves, reminiscent of a piazza where sun worshipers and people watchers can lounge in casual indolence.

Behind and to the side of the steps are urns and fountains, while the midsection is occupied by the gold-leafed, bronze statue of Alma Mater—on her lap a book, in her upraised right hand a crowned scepter, a kingly reminder of the school's origins. Daniel Chester French would design more sculptures after this masterpiece. But none would be more noble, none more dignified, none more appropriate.

Appellate Court Building

This view does scant justice to the aesthetics and dignity of the Appellate Court Building—utilitarian yet beautiful, solid and pronounced yet graceful, almost fluid.

Completed in 1899, the modest-sized three-story structure was the design of architect James Brown Lord, who was selected by the justices who would occupy the building themselves. This manner of selection procedure wherein the residents of a civic structure are permitted to choose their own builder—and that without the necessity of even holding a competition—is highly irregular. Fortunately, the results more than justified this particular selection, even though Lord's grandfather and father were practicing attorneys in a well-known law firm: well-known by the justices.

Much has been made of the building's sculptures and statuary. This is as it should be; though not greatly larger than life-size, the statues dominate the structure. Religious, secular, and legal figures are represented, each presumably connected to some integral part of the law. The image of Solon, the great Athenian lawgiver, was executed by the masterful hands of Herbert Adams. From here we may go down the list of statuary: Lycurgus by George Edwin Bissell; Zoroaster by Edward

Clark Potter; Justinian, the work of Henry Kirke Bush-Brown; Manu, by Henry Augustus Lukeman; Alfred the Great, rendered by Jonathan Scott Hartley; Confucius by the well-known Phillip Martiny; St. Louis of France by John Donoghue; and Justice, wrought by the stylist Daniel Chester French. A further statue, that of Mohammed by Charles Albert Lopez, was removed when the building was renovated in 1954, because of Muslim protest against the statue's presence.

All of this statuary resides above the cornice.

Also attached to the outside of the building, besides the masterful Corinthian columns purposefully elongated and set on tall bases to make the structure itself appear larger, are a pediment sculpture by Charles Niehaus, an allegorical representation of the Triumph of Love; above that, Daniel Chester French's statuary grouping of Justice, Study, and Power; Frederick Ruckstuhl's seated figures of Wisdom and Strength, which flank the Twenty-fifth Street entrance; and four caryatids topping the Corinthian portico on Madison Avenue, the work of Thomas Shields Clarke; above which is yet another figural grouping, entitled *Peace,* by Karl Bittner.

Architect Lord had given his artists a long leash, with

the solo provision that their finished products be in the neoclassical tradition. Obviously, his artistic largesse paid big dividends.

The Court House's interior is only slightly less elaborate in ornamentation. Siena marble, stained glass, and onyx paneling complement the lovely murals that decorate the building's walls. The stained-glass dome, which was designed by Martland Armstrong, is a gorgeous topping, below which delicate allegorical panels and murals are flanked by colonnettes. Fluted marble piers and Corinthian pilasters divide into bays the walls of the main hall, which serves as lobby and waiting room. The glass chandelier is an overhead complement; what sits underneath, including leather-covered Herter Brothers chairs and carved wood ornamentations, would be impressive by any standards.

Call it English Classical. Call it Neoclassical. Call it Palladian Revival. Or simply call it magnificent.

Lower Falls, Bronx Park

Lower Falls, Bronx Park, N. Y.

Since the days of "Rough-Riding" president Theodore Roosevelt, and certainly in keeping with his inclinations and efforts, America has had an ongoing love affair with zoos, parks, and museums of natural history.

Roosevelt may have shot and killed the large African beasts, but he also admired and respected them. This same mind-set seems to apply to many other Americans, especially when it comes to the truly large mammals.

Bigger and better are two words that also apply to the world-renowned Bronx Zoo. Alternately called the New York Zoological Society, the Bronx Zoo is the largest urban facility of its kind in America. It contains over four thousand animals, some housed in early-twentieth-century buildings, others allowed to roam over the 265-acre expanse of natural habitats created for them. These include Wild Asia, inhabited by elephants, rhinoceros, gibbons, sika deer, and others; the Himalayan Highlands, colorfully populated by red pandas and snow leopards; and a World of Darkness, with its denizens of bats and other creatures of the night.

And this is only the beginning. The World of Birds, the Reptile House, Jungle World, the African Plains; there is also a Children's Zoo, where the kids can try on a turtle shell or climb a spiderweb.

Two-Horned African Rhinoceros

Founded in 1895, the Bronx Zoo has long been a model for other urban zoos to emulate. The goal of its founders—to establish a home environment so that "captive animals" would be "not only comfortable but really happy" as well—has come very close to realization. Medical facilities as good as those for humans are offered for any and all maladies and illnesses that may befall any of the hundreds of species of animal life at the zoo.

Research into animal behaviors, animal illnesses and pathologies, animal intelligence, animal socialization, and other areas of animal life are continually being explored, examined, and painstakingly researched at the facility.

Teddy Roosevelt would be happy, proud, and surprised by what he would see at the zoo. New Yorkers, decidedly more blasé, would probably brag that they have the best lion or dog houses in the world.

They might be right.

Post Office, Brooklyn

Post Office, Brooklyn, N.Y.

For anyone with an appreciation of the past, especially as it relates to architectural splendor, New York City represents a multifaceted encounter with the sublime.

The churches, the castlelike residences, what remains of the Old World–style hotels, the train stations, the restaurants, the cemeteries, the parks: All of these include their bevy of architectural and historical beauties.

Even the civic and government buildings, like Brooklyn's Cadman Plaza General Post Office, built between 1885 and 1891. Seldom has the Romanesque Revival style been used to better effect in a public building. This postcard view is one instance in which a picture is indeed worth a thousand words. Or more.

The good news is that the structure proudly stands, victor against the city's pollution and the ravages of more than a hundred winters, more than a century of summers.

Hoagland Laboratory

HOAGLAND LABORATORY, L.I. COLLEGE HOSPITAL, BROOKLYN, N.Y.

Even on this pre-1920 viewcard, Hoagland Laboratory seems more than slightly out of place. Small wonder: The Romanesque Revival building, with its ivy-decorated exterior, looks as if it would be more at home in a seventeenth-century setting than in a twentieth-century one.

A part of Long Island College Hospital, Hoagland Laboratory, built in 1888, was the first privately founded laboratory in the country devoted to histological, bacteriological, and pathological research.

Partially destroyed by fire, the laboratory was later demolished. Of special mention were its wondrous art-nouveau-style copper signs.

Cortlandt Street

Copyright 1905 by the Rotograph Co.
G 185 a Cortlandt St., East from P. R. R. Ferry, N. Y. City. *Edward*
12/11/05 - *foots a Hudson River*

One of the many names familiar to students of New York City history is that of Van Cortlandt, who came to New Amsterdam in 1638. The dynasty that he started was an influential one that achieved its status—and made its money—through a combination of hard work, ingenuity, and marrying into the right families. At one time the Cortlandt family owned almost two hundred square miles of land, making it a (not surprising) fact that one of the city's streets would carry their name.

Among their contributions to New York's historical legacy are the Van Cortlandt Mansion and Van Cortlandt Park, the city's third-largest park setting. Both are in the Bronx.

The mansion, a square Georgian fieldstone-and-brick affair, has double-hung windows (the principal ones having carved heads above), dormer windows for that gabled look, a U-shaped staircase in the front hall, and beautiful settings of early-English and -American furniture. The mansion has been maintained as a museum since 1897 by the National Society of Colonial Dames.

Van Cortlandt Park is a grand getaway without apologies. Nor does it need them. Its more than eleven hundred acres of inviting greenery, walking trails, and playgrounds can accommodate baseball, soccer, cricket, football, tennis, and swimming—and golf as well, the park maintaining the nation's oldest municipal golf course. Its lake is well stocked with fish. A look at the Old Putnam Railroad Track and the Cass Gallagher Nature Trail are trips back in time from the nineteenth-century Track to the prehistoric Ice Age Trail.

Roxy Theatre

ROXY THEATRE · NEW YORK CITY

Samuel Lionel Rothafel (aka "Roxy") was the man primarily responsible for the erection of the International Music Hall (later called Radio City Music Hall by David Sarnoff) and the RKO Roxy (also later changed to Center Theater, as a result of a lawsuit by Roxy Theatre). Rothafel, whose entrepreneurial reputation was already secure in the vaudeville and movie business, had recommended the construction of Radio City and the Center as accoutrements to the RCA Building itself, which they flanked.

Roxy himself had already built, in 1927, the world's largest movie theater (seating capacity almost six thousand) on Fifteenth Street between Sixth and Seventh avenues. Named—what else?—the Roxy, it featured the Roxyettes, who were to become—(again, what else?)—Radio City's ever-famous Rockettes.

Madison Square

3033 Madison Square, 23d Street & Broadway, N. Y. City.

Madison Square is yet another one-time location where the wealthy hobnobbed, decorating themselves with finery just as they embellished their opulent homes. The Square was, in fact, an area where the elegantly famous "Four Hundred" cavorted, often led by one Roosevelt or another, dining and dancing at the likes of Delmonico's.

It wasn't always that way. Originally named—if indirectly—for President Madison, the site was previously used as a pauper's burial ground, a potter's field where were interred the remains of scarlet-fever victims. It was later an arsenal, then the location for a House of Refuge (built for youthful delinquents, the House was destroyed in fire in 1839). An infamous tavern on the spot was razed in 1852 to make way for Franconi's Hippodrome, and later the well-known Fifth Avenue Hotel.

Officially opened in 1847, Madison Square Park was the scene of the first professional baseball game in 1845. Two years earlier the renowned Knickerbocker Club had been formed by a group of gentlemen needing some exercise; they promptly made up a rudimentary set of rules, and baseball was born.

Within the environs of the Madison Square District were several structures either architecturally delightful or historically significant. These included the Madison Square Presbyterian Church, which had green granite columns, a pillared portico, and a dome reminiscent of Rome's Pantheon, and D. H. Burnham and Company's Fuller Building (nicknamed the Flatiron Building for its wedge shape)—286 feet and 21 stories of elaborately decorated limestone (to the fourth floor) and terra-cotta. Erected in 1902, the Renaissance Revival building is considered New York's first true skyscraper. The Manhattan Club, headquarters for Democratic leaders, is rumored to have been the place where the Manhattan cocktail was invented. The glamorous Fifth Avenue Hotel was a watering hole and meeting place for elites from the Republican Party. Completed in 1859, the hotel succeeded also as a center of social life even beyond the Gilded Age. One could also find a replicated version of Theodore Roosevelt's birthplace, now a museum administered by the National Park Service; the Metropolitan Life Insurance Company Building (rising 617 feet) and the Tower, now used for office rental space; and, on a smaller scale, the home for the American Society for the Prevention of Cruelty to Animals, opened in 1866, begun by humanitarian Henry Bergh. Finally, there are the masterful Appellate Court Building; an obelisk-shaped memorial to Mexican War hero General William Jenkins Worth; and the Eternal Light, a burning star on top of a flagpole, erected to commemorate the American Expeditionary Forces who fought in France during World War I. There was also, of course, the original Madison Square Garden.

Mention should be made, as well, of Madison Square's statuary. In addition to the Eternal Light Flagpole (the work of Carrere and Hastings) are the following: a statue of David Farragut (1880), first American admiral, excellently sculpted by Augustus Saint-Gaudens (his first major commission), with the pedestal under the supervision of Stanford White; another Chester A. Arthur, by George E. Bissell (1899), somewhat less imposing than Saint-Gaudens's work, but a quality statue nonetheless. The sadness on Arthur's face is the look one would expect on the countenance of a vice president who had to assume the presidency after his superior's (James A. Garfield's) assassination. There is also an interesting statue of William Seward, by Randolf Rodgers (1876). The seated figure was originally a statue of Abraham Lincoln, but inadequate funding curtailed that project. Seward's head took the place of Lincoln's, but the Emancipation Proclamation in his hand remains intact.

Transportation Center, New York City

Transportation Center, New York City.

It is sometimes the case that great accomplishments take place in environments that do not lend themselves to ease of effort. Such was the situation involving the building of the world's greatest subway system, in New York City.

Begun by one man, the task was taken over by another. Started under one city government, it continued under others. Dreamed of by two men, it was completed by neither.

It is still unfinished.

The Pennsylvania Tunnels

The Pennsylvania Tunnels, New York.

Since midnineteenth century onward, New York was in increasingly desperate need of a rapid-transit system. The prevailing deplorable conditions included ever-worsening street overcrowding, undependable transport, and unsanitary street conditions. The horses that pulled carts, wagons, and carriages deposited tons of manure each day, making pedestrian travel hazardous, unpleasant, and unhealthy.

The creation of the El trains in the 1870s, which carried thousands of passengers on their tracks, was a marginal godsend only; the boon they offered in alleviation of traffic congestion was offset by the unbearable rumbling and clatter, the discomfort of the ride itself, and the pollution that the trains continually spewed out.

Boss Tweed and his Tammany Hall machine were willing to construct a transit system, but only on their terms, which meant that the enterprise would be padded with unnecessary expense, the project given to Tammany cronies, and the safety—or even the workability—of the system would be suspect.

Into this breech stepped a dreamer named Alfred Beach, a man willing to spend his own capital and energies on the creation of a "pneumatic" subway system.

Hudson and Manhattan Tubes

Hudson and Manhattan Tube.
New York City.

© by Brown Bros. N. Y.

inventors. His plan for solving New York's transportation problem was to construct a subway, London having already designed one for its people. Unlike the British model, which required the use of steam—with its attendant health problems—Beach proposed the use of huge fans to move the train forward, and to draw it back again.

The problem now became Tammany Hall; Boss Tweed was not averse to public transportation as long as his people did the work and his graft machine was allowed to operate in unfettered fashion. To Beach this was unacceptable. Instead, he wisely chose to interest the state legislature in his project by submitting his plan for a limited subway to be used for carrying freight rather than human cargo. The legislature gave its approval, but Beach found it necessary to complete his project surreptitiously, away from the prying eyes of omnipresent Tammany. This he accomplished by renting the basement of a clothing store, under which he had his construction crew begin the tunnel. All the work had to be done at night, which meant conditions were sometimes unsafe as a result of inadequate lighting, poor ventilation, and other problems.

The ironic twist to the project was to be found in the fact that the tunnel, which would extend one block along Broadway from Warren Street to Murray Street, was within shouting distance of City Hall.

After just fifty-eight nights of work, the tunnel was completed, ready to transport twenty-two people in the most luxurious coach imaginable. The opulent amenities included chandeliers, upholstered seats, a fountain, a grand piano, a grandfather clock, damask curtains, and a fish tank filled with colorful, frisky goldfish. Nor was the engineering itself of less than excellent quality. The tracks were solid, the tunnel's white-painted walls secure, the fans fully operational. The ride was described in glowing terms—smooth and flawless.

Discussion about building a safe, efficient, pollution-free rapid-transit system for New York City had taken place during the 1850s but no moves were made at that time to accommodate any of the ideas that had been presented.

The project, however, could not be forestalled much longer. The population of Manhattan was approaching 1 million and increasing rapidly.

What was needed was a man with both vision and technical expertise. That individual appeared in the 1860s: Alfred Beach, journalist and inventor, was a man whose reputation in the arena of mechanical science was solid and secure. But Beach was also a dreamer, as are most

Tammany, unlike the public, was not impressed. Tweed sniffed contemptuously, blocking Beach at every turn. Though the state legislature twice approved the project, Tammany's New York governor vetoed it each time. Beach had spent $350,000 on his model, $70,000 of which was his own money. But without state funding he could go no further. His attempts to raise money by renting out his train and tunnel first as a shooting gallery, then as a storage vault, only briefly forestalled the inevitable. The tunnel was eventually sealed shut, and with its demise was also lost any nineteenth-century hope for a mass-transit subway system.

It was arguably New York's most magnificent failure.

Pennsylvania Station

PENNSYLVANIA STATION, NEW YORK
MAIN WAITING ROOM,
LOOKING TOWARDS GRAND CONCOURSE

The 1888 blizzard that effectively shut down the city of New York made people realize that their town needed a rapid-transit system immune to this kind of catastrophe. Reform mayor Hewitt wasted no time proposing a rapid-transit railroad that same year.

By 1894 the Chamber of Commerce was ready to approve his suggestion. Yet there was opposition and there was fear, both occasionally comingling. People feared that the subway would either collapse what stood above it or ruin cherished structures like Trinity Church, which was on Broadway along the proposed route. Moreover, some believed that the construction work itself would disrupt business and impede traffic; even those less cautious were concerned that the pounding and clatter might have the earthquake effect of causing buildings to sway and possibly to topple.

But Boston had already built a subway, proving that it could be done without major disruption. Additionally, the idea of a subway had gained acceptance in major sections of New York society, which not only realized the need for an efficient subway system, but also desired that the city, as befitted its size and importance, deserved the largest and best in America, if not in the world.

City Hall Subway Station

City Hall
Subway Station,
New York.

The three men most responsible for the building of the New York subway system were Mayor Hewitt; August Belmont, president of the Interborough Rapid Transit System (IRT); and William Parsons, the architect of the project.

Belmont, a multimillionaire financier, was willing to underwrite the work, even though it was generally believed in financial circles that anyone attempting the project was doomed to failure. Belmont thought dif-

ferently, as did Parsons, a Columbia graduate who had undertaken engineering projects around the world. He knew the undertaking would be the greatest in which he would ever be involved; consequently, Parsons was willing to dedicate his life to its successful completion.

Given the problems he would encounter, Parsons would eventually require every scrap of dedication and determination he could muster to finish his phase of the New York subway system.

Hudson Terminal and Tubes

9312 — Elevated Railroad on Bowery, New York

William Parsons's plans for the building of New York's subway (or Interborough Rapid Transit System) called for a twenty-one-mile route starting at City Hall, progressing up the east side of Manhattan to Grand Central Station, then crossing Forty-second Street and proceeding north, finally dividing into two tunnels heading under the Hudson River into the Bronx.

After investigating European subway systems, Parsons was led to believe—correctly, as it occurred—that electrical power rather than steam was the wave of the future. Electricity was used in lighting and in motor transport, including trains, even before the turn of

the century; thus Parsons stood on solid ground in his thinking.

More problematic was the construction of the underwater railroad tube tunnels, and also the erection of the other tunnels through Manhattan Island, that was a topographical nightmare of hills and valleys aboveground, its subterranean conditions including areas of quicksand, underground streams, and building foundations that had to be avoided.

Each of these difficulties was eventually conquered, but not without danger at too many turns and subsequent loss of life, the toll that this danger occasionally exacted.

Pennsylvania R. R. under the Hudson River

Pennsylvania R. R. under the Hudson River, New York City.

By the time of its grand opening in 1904, the Interborough Rapid Transit System had employed the services of more than seventy-seven hundred men over its four years of construction. First were the diggers who removed the dirt and mud, then the rock men, carpenters, and bricklayers, each laboring long hours during periods of heat and cold, always a bit enervated by the element of danger that accompanies such massive undertakings.

Purely in human terms, the world would have to look back to the building of the pyramids to find a comparison by numbers of laborers used on other construction projects.

A perfectionist by nature, Parsons personally oversaw as many aspects of the project as he could. No detail, from the composition of the gravel to the paint and the electrical generators, was overlooked. Dynamiting went on day and night, affecting not only everything aboveground that was not secured in some manner, but also the nerves of the citizens and workmen alike. These last were remunerated at rates from a low of $1.50 a day, to $6.00 per day for those in more dangerous positions, such as dynamiters and underwater tunnel workers.

In 1903 an accident occurred in which a large piece of falling rock resulted in the deaths of 3 workers. A later blast and subsequent fire killed 5 more and injured 125 others. All told, by 1904 there had been hundreds of accidents, both major and minor, resulting in thousands of injuries, with a total of 44 dead.

The world's largest and best subway system was not without cost on several fronts.

Long Island R.R. Station

Long Island R. R. Station, Brooklyn, N. Y.

Since 1904 the New York subway has seen additions that have increased it to 714 track miles linking every borough in the city, save Staten Island. Its 469 stations indicate that every area of Manhattan, Brooklyn, Queens, and the Bronx are within walking distance of a subway station.

The city is also serviced by a massive bus system, cabs, and limos for the rich and privileged. One wonders if their combined ridership is the equal of the subway, which annually carries over 1 billion bodies of human cargo.

One also wonders what it would have been like to ride a train departing from this station back in the days when comfort, not personal safety, was the primary area of concern.

173

CHAPTER 6

Lovers at Coney Island

We went down on the boat,
And while it was jay to float,
We both were happy when we got on dry land;
And now we'll never part
For I won her little heart
That sunday afternoon at Coney Island.

By the declining decades of the nineteenth century, the concept of "popular amusement" had firmly taken hold of western European consciousness. Following the precedent of the European trade fairs, centers of entertainment and commerce began to develop.

New York's Coney Island followed in that tradition, but it was easily and completely more grandiose. By 1904 Coney boasted several huge fun-filled parks with enticing names like Luna, Steeplechase, Sea Lion, and the fairy-tale-sounding Dreamland. Anything and just

short of everything in the way of diversion was seemingly available, all of it geared to separate the visitor from the contents of his or her pocketbook.

Clearly, Coney Island did not invent sin and folly; just as clearly, Coney did its best to make frivolous activity everyone's course of action.

As this picture illustrates, Coney's multiple rides, excursions, and plethora of fanciful sights also operated, on occasion, in the realm of romance.

Coney Island Express

Lying at the base of Brooklyn, Coney Island was originally little more than a bathing beach dotted with several hotels and a few chowder stands, until the 1870s. During that decade three prominent hotels—the Manhattan Beach, the Oriental, and the Brighton Beach—added a taste of splendor to the area skyline. Later a yellow-eyed, elephant-shaped hotel, replete with a dance hall, joined the carousels, as well as the Brazilian and Japanese pavilions coming directly from the U.S. Centennial Exhibition, which had just completed a successful showing in Philadelphia.

For all that, the island was still seen by the more respectable citizenry as little more than a stench-filled habitation on the order of Sodom and Gommorah.

"Sin debauched and crime soaked" railed Thomas Tully, secretary of the Law and Order Society.

What Coney Island had yet to acquire was an international reputation. This it did under the direction of George Tilyou, who made the island the world's number-one amusement haven, temporary destination of the young, the old, the rich, the poor, the social well-to-do and the ne'er-do-well.

With Tilyou came Steeplechase Park in 1897. With Steeplechase and all its attendant glory of sights, sounds, rides, and frights, the public persona of mad and wonderful Coney Island began to emerge.

Henderson's, Coney Island

HENDERSON'S | OPEN ALL YEAR | RESTAURANT
CONEY ISLAND. | | MUSIC HALL
Aug. 26, 1914.

It is difficult for anyone under the age of ninety to imagine the elegance and glamour one could find in a number of the eating establishments at Coney Island in the early 1900s.

"Open All Year," Henderson's Restaurant and Music Hall combined tastefulness with theatrical glitz and glitter. The dining rooms featured linen cloths and fine table settings, while the Music Hall's comic opera company played to packed houses of appreciative audiences.

Fred Henderson had come to Coney in the 1880s as a successful restaurateur. Unafraid to open his wallet, Henderson was precisely the type of capitalist businessman who could prosper in Coney's early twentieth-century environment.

As Henderson proved, visitors were willing to pay well for good food and family entertainment.

Culver and C. I. Brooklyn R.R. Station

Culver and C. I. Brooklyn R. R. Station, Coney Island, N. Y.

Before the first decade of the twentieth century was completed, Coney Island had attained a popularity that was extraordinary by any measure. Train stations like the Culver and C. I. Brooklyn, shown here, carried hundreds of thousands of passengers a day into and out of Coney.

While there, they could feast upon expensive cuisine in decorous settings, or savor the more common fare of a hot dog purchased from its professed creator, Charles Feltman, a gentleman of German extraction with hearty work habits to prove his Teutonic heritage.

Of course, the choice of cuisine was considered of less importance than the choice of what to see, or what to do. And here the choices were of the exhilarating variety. As might be expected, roller coasters abounded: A three-rail coaster called The Rough Riders was manned by men in Spanish-American War uniforms, while another coaster covered terrain constructed to represent the Swiss Alps.

But this was tame fare compared with spectacles like Brighton Beach's Boer War enactment, featuring real soldiers commanded by the old Boer general, Piet Arnoldus Cronje. Cronje had seen duty at the St. Louis World's Fair of 1904 and later performed his surrendering act at Coney for a season.

You're My Baby

Romance was a commodity in full supply at Coney, and proprietors of the various establishments on the Island were not loath to use it as an advertising inducement.

Al Ferguson's Band, which played at Stauch's Ballroom, did so to full houses. Stauch's claim that his ballroom contained the world's largest dance floor might have been questionable. That the music and dancing were incredibly popular is not. Even if one were dancing the "Grizzly Bear" to "You're My Baby."

Stauch's Restaurant and Dance Hall

Stauch's Restaurant & Dance Hall,
Coney Island, N. Y.

This postcard reflects a shadow only of the opulence that was Stauch's Restaurant and Dance Hall, one more mute testament to the fact that gaudiness and glamour existed cheek-to-jowl at Coney Island.

The facade of Stauch's was as impressive as that of a Fifth Avenue hotel, nor did the interior suffer with the same comparison. Decorated ceilings, fancy imported chandeliers, a tobacco department superior to most, a ball room with balcony (the dance floor could accommodate three thousand couples)—Stauch's would have been a formidable presence in any neighborhood.

Stauch himself had come to Coney in the 1870s and remained there both day and night throughout his life, never spending a single night away from the Island. It was reported that he even spent his honeymoon there.

Surf Avenue, Coney Island

Surf Avenue, Coney Island, N.Y.

Surf Avenue, Coney's main street, was surely the most absorbing piece of pavement in all creation. On each side were entrances to the colorful parks and dozens upon dozens of rides, fast-food establishments, and shows of every description. Add to this the multiple fun houses, penny arcades, games of chance, carousels, shooting galleries, waxworks, and tea rooms, and the image of a self-contained city comes to mind.

Down this thoroughfare, this incredibly busy thoroughfare, came the throngs of humanity seeking pleasure, romance, diversion. And they kept coming day in and day out, night in and night out, some staying until the two A.M. closing time.

Early every morning, before the crowds began their descent upon Surf Avenue, came the cleaners and delivery people, picking up refuse and resupplying shrunken stores of food, trinkets, and whatever else Coney provided in abundance.

Coney Island, Surf Avenue

Coney Island, Surf Avenue

Our nostalgic impression of a calmer, saner world in the early twentieth century is belied by the existence of places like Coney Island. If there is a "lowest common denominator," Coney would surely have represented that mathematical verity.

Walking down Surf Avenue was like meandering through the midway of a large state fair. At hand were delights to be grasped; in the distance would be fur-

ther awaiting delights. In between were the scents of popcorn and cotton candy, the odors of frankfurters and corn on the cob.

The jostling, the interminable waits in line, and the continuing sounds of mechanical contrivances in perpetual motion were a constant strain on the nerves, endured only because the anomaly of Coney Island rendered it all an experience not to be missed.

The Galveston Flood

CARTER & GUT, PUBLISHERS, N. Y.

SCENE FROM THE STUPENDOUS REPRODUCTION OF THE GREAT TIDAL WAVE
THE GALVESTON FLOOD
AT CONEY ISLAND, OPPOSITE CULVER DEPOT
SHOWING A SMALL PORTION OF THE IMMENSE SCENE OF THE CITY OF GALVESTON, AFTER THE FLOOD

182

What it is in humanity's psychological makeup that attracts us to the scene of a fire, a flood, or an automobile accident may perhaps never be fully understood. But the showmen and promoters at Coney Island must have been amateur psychologists of a sort to be able to tap into that fright-viewing mindset with such economic success.

The Galveston Tidal Wave, which killed seven thousand people, was reenacted before enthusiastic, if mortified, viewers on a daily basis. Obviously, picture-postcard publishers were not averse to turning a profit from human disaster. This card is a scenic panorama of the reenactment.

Shooting the Chutes

362   Shooting The Chutes, Luna Park, Coney Island, N. Y.

If period literature is to be believed, none of the rides at Old Coney Island enjoyed the popularity of Shoot the Chutes, an excursion that sees its modern counterpart in the innumerable Log Flume rides at innumerable amusement parks from Ohio's Kings Island to Six Flags over Texas.

The object of the ride—as with all rides—was to get from point A to point B, the former position in this instance being the top of an elongated slide down which one descended in pell-mell fashion while being situated within the confines of a flat-bottomed boat. Point B was the pool into which the boat cascaded, sending water flying in all directions, much of it drenching the boat's passengers.

Shrieks rent the air, whitened knuckles gripped the sides of the boat, and lips formed themselves alternately into smiles and grimaces; then, water-soaked clothes stuck to skin and water-plastered hair stuck to head, the rider might contemplate another slide down the watery Babylon.

Captain Paul Boynton, creator of Sea Lion Park and Coney's first user of Shoot the Chutes, had unfettered the zaniness in millions of riders. And along the way, no doubt, incurred their gratitude for all the times the trip would be relived in blissful memories.

General View, Tozman Plaza

PUB. BY SOUVENIR POST CARD CO. N.Y.

GENERAL VIEW TOZMAN PLAZA
MIDGET CITY, DREAMLAND, CONEY ISLAND

As that consummate showman P. T. Barnum demonstrated in the late nineteenth century with the diminutive Tom Thumb, midgets are a big draw for the curious-minded. Which pretty much means all of us.

Dreamland's Midget City met that curiosity more than halfway. Within the confines of the tiny community was a midget police force, a miniature fire department, a music hall, and a circus. The fire department was summoned often to the delight of more normal-sized spectators.

Midget City's three hundred pint-sized inhabitants included the widow of Tom Thumb. She was then married to "Count" Magri but chose the name Mrs. General Tom Thumb over that of Countess Magri.

Rolling Chairs on the Boardwalk, Coney Island

ROLLING CHAIRS ON THE BOARDWALK, CONEY ISLAND, N. Y.

Coney may not have invented the Boardwalk, but it certainly went some distance toward popularizing it. The crowds pictured here were typical. Throngs of walkers and rolling chair riders traveled part or all of Coney Island's two-mile stretch of wooden street.

From the Boardwalk visitors could view the entire beach or turn their heads elsewhere to see the public baths, the splendor of the Hotel Brighton, numerous fast-food eateries, stands where games of chance beckoned—and off in the distance, always off in the distance, the shrieks and shouts of fascinated park goers riding the rides, ogling the frights, part and parcel of the occasional thrills and chills.

Bathers' Delight at Coney Island

Bathers' Delights at Coney Island, N. Y.

Even with all the mechanical rides, the fun houses, and the grand spectacles, there was no escaping the fact that Coney Island was first, last, and foremost a beachfront property.

For as long as there have been large bodies of water, there have been large bodies of people with a desire to frolic or relax in them. On any given summer day Coney played host to thousands of visitors availing themselves of the beach or enjoying themselves in one of the numerous bathing pavilions on the grounds.

Actually, description is unnecessary: This picture says it all.

On the Sands of Coney Island

On the Sands of Coney Island.

Expect to be back Friday, the 30th. Hope you are all well. F. A. Gornely.

Rivaling the popularity of the French Riviera and other well-established spas, Coney Island's beaches and bathhouses were always crowded when weather permitted. As is evident from this postcard, not a few of the patrons could be seen sporting the latest fashions in swimwear and bathing attire.

Many went to the beach to be seen; more went to see. But the largest group were those who went to get wet by swimming, wading, or just putting their feet into the welcoming water.

187

Feltman's, Coney Island

The most well-known and most well-frequented eating establishment at Old Coney was Feltman's.

Charles Feltman, a one-time street vendor and man of vision, came to Coney with an idea: reasonably priced cuisine, pleasing both to the masses and to those with more discriminating tastes. His one staple was the hot dog, which he is often credited with inventing.

But a man of Feltman's capitalistic tendencies and modest economic genius could not long be satisfied with owning merely another mundane eatery.

By 1910, the year of his death, Feltman was serving almost a million customers a year. His once-small restaurant had by then grown into an establishment that housed a movie theater, a dance hall, a series of carousels, and a roller coaster called the *Zig* that sped back and forth among the trees on his grounds.

No small thinker he, Feltman had upgraded his cuisine as well, to include lobster, clam, crab, and steak. Remaining true to his origins, however, he made sure his restaurant contained seven grills in continual use preparing hot dogs for an ever-waiting audience of chomping enthusiasts.

Steeplechase Park

PUB. BY
PHOTO & ART P. C. CO., N. Y.

BOWERY AND STEEPLE CHASE
CONEY ISLAND.

If one man can be credited with creating the foundation and atmosphere that made possible the Coney Island of popular imagination, the Coney of games, rides, glitter, and effervescence, that man would be George C. Tilyou. Developing early on a desire to excel and a vision that matched that desire, drumbeat for drumbeat, Tilyou was the architect of Steeplechase Park, its fifteen acres crammed by thirty-one rides, a ballroom, and a five-acre pavilion, replete with hardwood floors and multiple mechanical contrivances to shake, spin, and otherwise rattle the rider.

By 1914, when Tilyou died, he had witnessed the emergence of even larger parks than his and seen Coney Island approach the pinnacle of its popularity. (That zenith was reached after World War I, when the New York subway arrived at Coney.)

But Tilyou had built the first of the big parks and therewith laid the blueprint for what was to follow. He led the way toward establishing Coney's raucous, romantic atmosphere. Steeplechase Park, with its giant seesaw, its oversize swimming pool, its Ferris wheel and Airship Ride, was amusement writ large and with a capital A, and thousands poured themselves daily into its sausage grinder of fun.

View of the Bowery, Coney Island

Few places had the independent flavor of New York's Bowery district. Nickel beer and twenty-five-cent palm readers vied with games of chance, street-side fast-food venders, and rickety rides for the visitor's money. This type of variety represented an adventure to all who strayed into the area.

Cheap women and cheaper booze thrived in this exciting Sodom, where calliopes blared music to step to, and the smell of tobacco was omnipresent. Dancing pavilions offered a chance at romance, again on the cheap. And even if it was not an enduring kind of love, and even if the eateries offered palate-pleasing but stomach-churning food, people could take consolation in two facts: They had survived a trip to the Bowery and—what the hey!—they had actually had some un-choreographed, spontaneous fun.

Miniature Railroad, Coney Island

NO. 176   THE MINIATURE RAILROAD, DREAMLAND.
PUB. BY I. STERN, BROOKLYN, N.Y.   . CONEY ISLAND.

Coney Island's Dreamland Amusement Park was an invigorating montage of visual delights. From the 375-foot central tower, gleaming and glaring white (as were most of Dreamland's structures), to Bostock's Animal Circus, to Midget City, to Hellgate, with its fiendish plaster apparatus staring down in sinister fashion from the entrance: All were intended to mesmerize.

The entrance to Dreamland itself might be variously described. The allegorical female figure, face turned to the side but breasts very much exposed, could be viewed as either aesthetically pleasing or as somewhat too vulgar and garish for morally sensitive or refined tastes.

The Miniature Railroad pictured there was located in Dreamland. Each of Coney's parks had its own small train capable of pulling several passenger tons at the speed of ten miles per hour. The rides were as much a success at early Coney as they were later to be at amusement parks and vacation spots around the world.

Coney Island's Biggest Fire Disaster

CONEY ISLAND'S BIGGEST FIRE DISASTER
DREAMLAND AFTER COMPLETE DESTRUCTION
SURF AVENUE LOOKING EAST··

The night before Memorial Day weekend of 1911 was the most memorable period in Coney Island history. For it was during this time that Dreamland, that angelic vision of painted purity around which popular songs had been composed, burned to the ground without a remaining trace of its otherworldly countenance. White on white became black on black, dismal on dismal.

Caged animals shrieked or snarled at the flames. Some died, some were rescued, some escaped the confines of Dreamland to run terrified and terrifying into the streets.

Four hundred men, including the Midget Fire Depart-ment squad, battled the flames during the early-morning hours, finally stopping the fire's forward progress at New York's West Fifth Street.

Six seasons had elapsed since Dreamland's grand opening. Coney had survived and would continue with some vestiges of dignity through the Second World War, but the Dreamland fire was an early precursor of Coney's slow demise beginning in the late twenties.

Paradise or hell—or a bit of both—came to New York, not as a permanent fixture, but as a temporary, flamboyant, and fiery painting on the skyline. Paradise or hell—or a bit of both—took down the gaudy display but left the electric impact and the memory intact.

CHAPTER 7

Riders of the Elements, New York World's Fair

"Riders of the Elements"

New York World's Fair 1939

A-38

By 1939 the concept of world's fairs on American shores was almost half a century old, the first such affair of international prominence being the Columbian Exposition held in Chicago in 1893.

Strange as it now seems, New York did not sponsor a world's fair until a number of these extravaganzas had first taken place elsewhere. However, when that exposition did finally occur in 1939, New York used the occasion to introduce eclectic statuary, such as that seen here—and marvels of technology soon to be gracing homes all over the Western World.

Trylon and Perisphere

59 W   Trylon and Perisphere, New York World's Fair

© N. Y. W. F.

Dubbed "The World of Tomorrow" by promoters, the 1939 New York World's Fair emphasized the world of technology. The seven-hundred-foot-high Trylon was linked by a bridge to the two-hundred-foot Perisphere. Symbolizing the twin ideas of progress and aspiration, these structures also represented the modernity and functional character of the architecture of all the fair's buildings.

The Trylon served both as a fair beacon and a broadcasting tower, while the fountain beneath the Perisphere created a wizard's illusion of a huge ball float-ing in midair, mute testament to the wonders of the future. The clusters of water that screened the piers supporting the Sphere made that great ball appear to be poised on jets of water. Ticket holders could view it from a revolving platform suspended above the ground.

New York's ebullient, irrepressible mayor, Fiorello La Guardia, could not have been more pleased by the spectacle as he went about the business of touting and promoting, promoting and touting. On the premises, no less: La Guardia was himself still a child at heart.

The Food Building

9A-H147

195

Food Building Number Two, seen here, occupied an acre-and-a-half site at the fair. Inside the circular dome were products from the American Food Service Industry, while the exterior colorful mural dramatized the housing of foodstuffs.

Here again, the architecture follows modern lines—that is, it demonstrates a daring break with Victorian embellishment, being more reminiscent of art-deco lines and overall stylization.

Ford Motor Company Building,
New York World's Fair

New York World's Fair 1939

FORD

FORD

116:—THE FORD MOTOR COMPANY BUILDING.

Although it had been almost two centuries since New York City could lay claim to being the nation's capital, pride among the citizenry could still be taken in the fact that George Washington, the first U.S. Chief Executive, took his oath of office here.

The 1939 World's Fair was, among other things, a celebration to commemorate the 150th anniversary of that event. But this fair chose to spend most of its resources pointing to the future rather than living in the past.

The Ford Motor Company Building illustrated here furnished an excellent example of U.S. technology at work.

A half-mile highway called The Road of Tomorrow, which rose upon a series of spiral ramps, circled the main building at the top of the walls after traversing the borders of a patio. Ford's new V-8's and Lincoln-Zephyrs were on display, and visitors were permitted to ride them on the elevated highway. More mundane sights, such as demonstration of Ford's mass-production methods, were also available. All of it pointed to a more efficient and faster-paced—if somewhat more impersonal—future for the Western World.

Zucca's Restaurant

The World Renowned Zucca's Restaurant, New York

VISIT THE NEW YORK WORLD'S FAIR 1939

Cuisine at the 1939 fair ran along the lines of what one might expect. Within the 1,216 acres of the exposition was the staple fare of palate-pleasing but often nutritionless fast food that one expects at such venues. Hot dogs and hamburgers, aroma-intoxicating shish kebabs, cotton candy and the like, were ubiquitously available. Scattered about, dotted across the Queen's landscape like autumn leaves scattered by a gust of wind, were more upscale establishments featuring more expensive epicurean delights.

New York mayor Fiorello La Guardia's claim that a family of four might be fed at the fair for the paltry sum of $1.50 defied credibility.

By 1939 American business had made a resounding comeback from the Great Depression, and prices on everything, food included, were beginning to escalate. Zucca's Restaurant at 118 West Forty-ninth Street was still selling chicken cutlet milanaise for one dollar on the luncheon menu ($1.50 for dinner), but prices would double during World War II and continue to climb thereafter.

As for the fair goers—especially those in attendance for only a brief span of time—eating was often an impromptu affair, engaged in between sightseeing and just pain ogling.

Railroad Exhibit Building

New York World's Fair 1939

114:—RAILROAD EXHIBIT BUILDING.

Within a quarter century of this date, U.S. railroads would be in dire economic straits, caused both by the burgeoning semitrailer truck business and the inefficiency of the railroad companies themselves.

But in 1939 the future of train travel looked sufficiently promising to justify the railroad display seen here, which was the largest private-exhibit building at the fair. Thirty-eight hundred feet of track in the back of the building was used to showcase the railroad's utility in transporting almost any kind of item imaginable, while a large model railroad operated for thirty-minute periods in front of a theater seating one thousand persons.

All told, twenty-seven railroads shared the cost and the attendant glory of a railway system, which was, in the late 1930s, the best and most complex the world had ever seen.

Or probably ever would see.

Bibliography

1. Berenholtz, Richard. *Manhattan Architecture.* New York: Prentice Hall, 1988.
2. Breeze, Carla. *New York Deco.* New York: Rizzoli International Publications, 1993.
3. Diamonstein, Barbaralee. *The Landmarks Of New York.* New York: Harry N. Abrams, 1988.
4. Federal Writers Project. *WPA Guide to New York City.* New York: 1939.
5. Gillon, Edmund Vincent. *Beaux-Arts Architecture in New York.* Text by Henry Hope Reed. New York: Dover Publications, 1988.
6. Goldberger, Paul. *The City Observed: New York.* New York: Random House, 1979.
7. Greene, Lisa M. *New York for New Yorkers.* New York: W. W. Norton, 1995.
8. Reynolds, Donald M. *The Architecture of New York City.* New York: Macmillan, 1984.
9. Robinson, Cervin. *Skyscraper Style, Art Deco New York.* New York: Oxford University Press, 1975.
10. Snow, Richard. *Coney Island, A Postcard Journey to the City of Fire.* New York: Brightwaters Press, 1984.
11. Stein, R. Conrad. *America the Beautiful, New York.* Chicago: Childrens Press, 1989.
12. Tauranac, John, and Christopher Little. *Elegant New York, The Builders and the Buildings 1885–1915.* New York: Abbeville Press, 1985.
13. Willensky, Elliot. *AIA Guide to New York City.* 3rd ed. San Diego: Harcourt Brace Jovanovich, 1988.

Index

201

203

204